Fishing the Flats

Fishing the Flats

Mark Sosin
and Lefty Kreh

NICK LYONS BOOKS
WINCHESTER PRESS

THE SALT WATER
SPORTSMAN LIBRARY

For
FRANK WOOLNER
who helped start us in this business
and was always there every inch of the way

Produced by
NICK LYONS BOOKS
212 Fifth Avenue
New York, NY 10010

Published and distributed by
WINCHESTER PRESS
New Century Publishers, Inc.
220 Old New Brunswick Road
Piscataway, NJ 08854

PRINTED IN THE UNITED STATES OF AMERICA

10 9 8 7 6 5 4 3 2 1

Library of Congress Cataloging in Publication Data

Sosin, Mark.
  Fishing the flats.

  "A Nick Lyons book."
  1. Saltwater fishing.   2. Tarpon fishing.
3. Bonefishing.   4. Fishing—Florida.
I. Kreh, Lefty.   II. Title.   III. Title: Flats.
SH457.3.S67   1983   799.1'6   82-20158
ISBN 0-8329-0278-0
ISBN 0-8329-0280-2 (paperback)

Contents

Introduction

by Hal Lyman and Frank Woolner

A HEART-STOPPING BULGE OF WATER BENEATH A DELI-
cate dry fly ghosting down a crystal stream sharpens every sense in the
dedicated trout fisherman. Pinpoint wader leaks, which allow an icy trickle of
water to cool his feet, are all but forgotten; hours of fruitless casting pass into
history. He has matched the hatch and the resulting reward is well worth the
wait, effort, and frustration.

Multiply that reward a hundredfold as far as size of quarry and expanse
of fishable littoral waters are concerned: this is the world of tidal flats—coral
heads and turtle grass in southern climes, shifting sands and barnacle-
encrusted boulders to the north. It is an angler's world where knowledge,
skill, and experience combine to convert the unwary fresh-water light-tackle
addict to the call of the sea. That first hooked tarpon, exploding into the air
with gill covers rattling, appears to be the size of a cow. The sizzling run of a
bonefish melts line off the reel at an express rate. Striped bass, normally
dogged underwater fighters, suddenly become cart-wheeling, aerial acrobats.

The flats themselves are feeding grounds as the rising tides stir many
nutrients from the bottom. They are also nursery grounds, not only for a
thousand forms of sea life but also for anglers moving from inland to the
coasts. Here the breath of salt air may change the craving for a whiff of
hemlock and spruce forever.

Flats fishermen, like their fresh-water counterparts, have hunter's blood
in their veins. They do not wait for their quarry: they stalk it as carefully as a
Highland Scot creeps up on a stag. Casting skills are honed to a fine edge and
tackle becomes a sensitive extension of hand and arm. When the sweet-water
angler turns toward the coasts, it is little wonder that he usually is initiated
into his new world on the shallows that extend for hazy miles. The game is
similar to that which he has played for years along river and lake shores, but it
is not the same.

This book describes the differences, details the tackle best used in thin
salt water, polishes techniques that have been proven on site. Angling of this
type may be considered unique in many ways; therefore this book is unique.
Although many articles about fishing the flats have been written since the late

George Bonbright tackled tarpon with a fly in the early twentieth century, this is the first volume that covers the whole shallow, watery world of marine angling and its multitude of species. And it covers it well.

Explanations for this excellence are easy: the two authors are masters of their varied crafts. We could retire in comfort if we had a dollar for every 100 yards Mark Sosin and Lefty Kreh have poled skiffs over the flats, searching for that telltale puff of mud raised by a feeding bonefish, a quick flash of silver as a tarpon turns briefly on its side, the black shadow of a cruising shark. Mark and Lefty are both superb fishermen—and light tackle is their specialty. Together they have created a book that will stand as a standard reference for many years to come.

Since before gray tinged our own locks, we have known them both and have watched with pleasure as they have scaled the rough cliffs to the upper plateaus of salt-water angling. Wherever writers, anglers, and photographers gather, the assembly is enlivened by Lefty's incredible fund of humor and often impudent stories of fishing gods with feet of clay. Mark has an encyclopedic knowledge of fish and fishing; do not challenge his facts unless you have a notarized text with which to back your arguments! Both love their sport and, as may be seen in all that follows, they dote on flats fishing as grandparents dote on their first grandchild.

Halieutics—the science and art of fishing—is our specialty. In this volume, you will find a specialty within that specialty—the skills and methods forged from experience that make fishing the flats an exciting adventure for even the most hard-bitten angler. There is nothing quite like it in the marine world.

No one lives forever. When Charon ferries us across the River Styx on our last watery trip, we will ask him to pause briefly over the flats at the seaward end of that murky current so that we may make just one more cast. To keep his mind off the pressing needs of other passengers, we plan to slip into his hands a much-thumbed and dog-eared copy of *Fishing the Flats*. Who knows? We may stay there for a happy eternity.

1 · The Flats

THE BRIGHT, BRUTAL SUN PIERCES THE WATER'S SUR-
face and illuminates the bottom with the intensity of a mammoth searchlight.
You are standing atop the casting platform of a specially designed skiff that
will float in a puddle, straining your eyes to scan the panorama of light and
shadow that stretches in every direction. Concentration becomes tension.
Your hand tightens around the rod grip and you rehearse the procedure for
the hundredth time.

When the fish finally show, it is with a suddenness. A moment before, the
flats seemed void of life. Now a school of fish that had looked like an indistinct
shading across the bottom is moving toward you. For an instant, you are
uncertain. Then, you realize that this is what it is all about. The first
presentation must be perfect. Excuses are a luxury and second chances do not
come often.

There are no parallels, no analogies, no comparisons, and no training
grounds in any other type of fishing. This is opportunity fishing at its finest,
where an angler can stalk his quarry with the skill and finesse of a hunter. The
shallow flats are unique and addictive. Not only do they draw the salt water
devotee like a powerful magnet but they also sing a siren's song to trout and
salmon purists and have the effect of a strong drug on bass and pike aficiona-
dos. Once sampled, the experience will never be forgotten and you can bet
that you will be back again and again and again.

The techniques you master in these very special waters will serve you
well wherever you choose to fish and for whatever species you decide to seek.
An angler who develops the skill to put a fly in front of a moving bonefish
discovers that he does much less false casting on a trout stream and has no
trouble dropping a hunk of hair or feathers upstream from a feeding brown.
Learn to wrestle a tarpon on light gear and you will do better with a
largemouth bass in a tangle of tree limbs.

Most of the light tackle innovations are developed and tested in the
shallows, where the fish are incredibly strong and particularly demanding.
Equally significant, everything happens right before your eyes. You know
when a fish rejects a lure and you can tell in an instant whether the tackle is

up to the task. Over the years, the pleas and urgings of the shallow-water enthusiast have prompted tackle manufacturers to improve their products. If gear can endure the torture tests of the flats, it can survive anywhere.

Flats form a specific estuarial ecosystem and are usually characterized by relatively level or gently sloping terrain. Sharp dropoffs are the exception. Some flats lie in the rich intertidal zone with vast portions exposed to the air or barely covered with water at low tide. Others, of course, are deeper. For this book, flats will mean areas that have 12 feet of water or less.

Because of the abundance of food in this constantly changing environment, game fish leave the sanctuary of the depths to search for a meal. To them, these shallow expanses represent the finest supermarkets with delicacies cramming every shelf. Thin water makes every fish skittish. They are out of their element and know it. Given a choice, these creatures would abandon the idea of prowling areas where the sea barely covers their backs, but they return day after day because that is where the food supply lives.

The surface can be deceptive. If you study the bottom contours, you know that flats are not smooth or even. Instead, they are a miniature maze of mountains and valleys, canyons and pockets, channels and plateaus. Some of these may be variations of only a few inches, others a couple of feet or more. The point to remember is that a subtle change of depth that could be spanned by the distance between your thumb and little finger may make the difference between finding fish and going fishless.

A man may sink to his waist instantly if he steps on certain bottoms, while other terrain is rock-hard. Flats may be formed from sand, coral particles, marl, mud, or rock. Turtle grass covers many areas and is often a key indicator that fish will be nearby. You will also find your quarry over flats that look as barren as the outside of a honeydew melon. These expanses of sand, however, are a haven for the ghost crab and a dozen varieties of shrimp.

In the tropics, most flats are as clear as the windshield on a new car. A few might be off-color or even muddy, but they're the exception. As latitude increases, shallow water becomes more turbid and visibility from the surface decreases significantly. Still, these areas are flats and must be fished with a special technique.

An expanse of flats may stretch uninterrupted for miles or it may be laced with deep finger channels that provide easy access for fish entering and leaving the shallows. Channels must be viewed as rivers that feed or drain the ecosystem and should be fished that way. Frequently, they serve as a home for the predators that climb the flats to feed.

From a fishing standpoint, a productive flat generally boasts a good tidal range with a strong flow, connects with deep water, and offers fish some type of cover or traveling routes. Abundant bird life on a flat indicates that bait is plentiful. Through close observation, one may also spot small fish such as pinfish, needlefish, boxfish, and other species on which predators feed. The

There's no greater angling thrill than to be poled across the flats in a specially designed skiff and cast directly to fish you can see. It's a one-on-one situation that has no parallel.

late Joe Brooks, who was a treasured friend, always insisted that the chances of catching fish were much improved if you could see an abundance of sharks and rays on a flat. The absence of activity is a warning to be suspicious.

One of the most difficult concepts for the newcomer is how shallow the water can be where big fish will be found. It is commonplace in some portions of Florida Bay, for example, to see 100-pound tarpon with their bellies rubbing the bottom and tails and dorsals cutting the surface. Bonefish will sometimes feed this way and the telltale V-wake of a shark whose back is getting a suntan is a sight to behold.

Shallows taper into deeper water. These edges, as they are called, become holding areas for those game fish that tend to work back and forth. Tarpon have a habit of shouldering the edges of basins as they swim so that the tide pushes them right up against a flat. They find food along these slight dropoffs and instinctively prowl that zone.

Bait, on the other hand, knows that the shallower it can get, the less chance a hungry predator has of catching it. Nature's endless struggle takes place in this marginal zone. When a fish is on the flats, it is there strictly to feed. That means if your offering is refused, something is wrong with it or the presentation was incorrect. A refusal indicates instantly that technique or lure needs refinement. And the whole process takes place right before your eyes; you see what happens rather than using your imagination.

THE SEASONS

Magazine tales and newspaper accounts that extol the glories of fishing the flats seldom emphasize the importance of seasons. People begin to think that the fish are there every month of the year regardless of conditions and are extremely disappointed when they discover, after their arrival, that the species they wanted will not show in any quantity for months.

Timing is critical. Being on the flats during the right season can be much more meaningful than hiring the best guide. Even the leading experts cannot manufacture fish. Therefore, we want to stress the significance of seasons. If you are a trout fisherman, you would not be at streamside in February looking for a mayfly hatch. Bass anglers would be hard-pressed to find their quarry on the beds in January. It's no different on the flats.

A number of factors govern the presence or absence of fish on the flats during a given season. In warm climates, water temperature is perhaps the most critical aspect. Keep in mind that shallow water warms much faster than the depths; it also cools with equal speed. Even tropical species of fish have temperature tolerances. There are minimums and maximums with which to contend.

Tarpon require a minimum temperature of 75° before they'll invade the flats. You can pole for miles and never see a fish in 73° water, but when the magic number is reached, the fish will appear. It is a mystery how they know that the flats have warmed, but it happens with regularity. Local experts recognize, for example, that a few warm, calm days during the winter will cause tarpon to flood into the backcountry of the lower Florida Keys. At the first sign of a cold snap, they're gone.

An angler casts a crab to a cruising permit.

This is a typically good bonefish flat. There's not too much water, plenty of mangroves surround and protect the shoreline, and the bottom has considerable turtle grass.

To demonstrate the effect of maximum temperatures, the habits of the bonefish serve as a case in point. As soon as the water temperature climbs above 85° in the summer, the gray ghost becomes much more difficult to find. Those that do appear are closer to deep water and tend to show early and late in the day.

Food supply is another major factor in the appearance of fish in the shallows. It too is affected by high and low temperatures. Some of the finest sport for big bluefish occurs in Chesapeake Bay and the bays of the North Carolina coast each spring when water temperatures in the shallows range between 64° and 72°. These fish are in three to five feet of water because the menhaden happen to prefer those conditions. Later in the season, smaller blues probe the shallows, but the husky fish are long gone.

Migratory habits constitute another influence on flats fishing. No one really has a handle on where tarpon spawn or the migratory patterns they follow. They appear first in the Dry Tortugas and then in Key West. Observers believe that the fish have moved across the Gulf of Mexico, but facts are sketchy. Then, as the weather warms and water temperatures rise, these big silver kings work their way up the chain of Keys.

The pattern becomes even more complex. Until May, virtually all of the tarpon in the Keys are found in the backcountry on the Gulf side. Sometime during that month, a gradual migration starts and the fish move to the ocean side. Far fewer fish remain in the Gulf. The fish in the Gulf have green-hued backs and silver sides, while tarpon in the Atlantic boast blue backs. The markings are that distinct.

Although one can find a few tarpon in Florida throughout the year, the best period for trophy fish and consistent fishing begins each spring and lasts through the middle of July. Weather patterns determine how early the fish will show. In recent years, serious record-seekers have made the pilgrimage to Florida's West Coast around Crystal River and Homasassa. These are open flats with generally tough fishing conditions. The prime month in this region is May.

Bonefish can be caught throughout the year in Florida and the Bahamas, but they are susceptible to cold fronts during the winter and extremely hot temperatures in the summer. Although experienced guides can find a few fish in 65° water, you'll do a lot better when the thermometer reads 70° to 85°. April and May are peak months for bonefishing from Biscayne Bay, which is the northern range of the fish, down through the Keys. During that period, there are relatively few windy fronts moving down the state and water temperatures remain relatively constant and comfortable. That is usually the time when the biggest fish are caught, because they are laden with roe or milt for spawning.

October and the first part of November can also be an excellent time for the gray ghost of the flats. Again, it is a matter of weather. That does not mean that professional guides cannot locate a few fish even under extremes, but if you have a choice, always time your trip to coincide with the prime season.

Permit are much more elusive than bonefish, but the same seasonal guidelines pertain to both fish. There is one exception. During June and part of July, permit tend to disappear from the flats and are seen over the reefs and wrecks in greater numbers. They move offshore to spawn during this period. If you have your heart set on catching a permit, concentrate your efforts during April and May and again in late September, October, and early November.

Finding mutton snapper on the flats presents an exciting challenge. They are difficult to fool, strong fish to battle, and a worthwhile catch. Pinpointing the patterns of their appearance is difficult if not impossible. However, they do show in late March and April on some flats. The theory is that they then go out to spawn.

Redfish prove to be most abundant from Texas to the southwest corner of Florida in the summer and through the fall. The reds are not as sensitive to water temperatures as other species. During the late spring and summer months, you will also find channel bass (big reds) on the inside flats along North Carolina's Outer Banks. When the weather turns cold in November and December, redfish off the Louisiana coast move into the deeper river holes in the marshes, but some bruising fish arrive late and the pass fishing in the shallows can be excellent.

The summer months represent a peak time for spotted seatrout from Texas through North Carolina, but the fishing extends into the fall of the year. In Florida, trout fishing hits its zenith in the spring and again in the fall, and some big "alligator trout" may be taken when the weather turns chilly.

If you are looking for heavyweight barracuda, fish the cold snaps during the winter months in the Florida Keys. That is when the toothy brutes really invade the shallows. Sharks, on the other hand, may be ferocious, but they are pussycats when it comes to water temperature. The big boys prowl the flats during the summer, but plummeting temperatures will keep them in deep water throughout other parts of the year.

On the West Coast, striped bass fishing begins to build in San Francisco Bay during August and continues in September, October, and part of November. Some really husky fish push through the shallows at that time and it is perhaps the best place to catch a trophy striper on light tackle.

Various flat areas along the Northeast Coast attract striped bass during the spring months with fewer fish scouting these areas in the fall. Bait and temperatures are the critical factors. In the spring, much of the food remains in the shallows because those waters warm faster. During the fall, much of the bait supply leaves the estuaries and filters down along the coast.

Spring is an excellent time to find weakfish on the flats in the north country. Certain places on New York's Long Island, for example, boast an abundance through June. There are also plenty of fish in Delaware Bay in May.

If you derive nothing else from this book, take the time to research the seasons for the species you seek and the region you intend to fish. It is obviously impossible to chart every area within the range of a given species, but you should ask a lot of questions before you commit to a time slot.

That advice is equally important outside the United States. The fact that a camp remains open is not a guarantee that the fishing will excel. Weather, such as the onset of the dry or rainy season, may be the determining factor in opening and closing a fishing camp. A few judicious inquiries should bring you the needed information.

Keep in mind that there are always exceptions to seasonal rules. Seasonal changes can come earlier or later in a given year. The weather patterns for the preceding several months can be important. If the winter was mild,

A well-designed fly rod, with the proper number of guides, will look like this when a heavy fish is lifted.

fish may be on the move earlier in the spring. A late arrival of the rainy season in another country may prolong the life of a fishery that normally would have ended.

Winter vacations in Florida provide an escape from the frigid blasts in the northern tier of states, but it is also winter down in the land of oranges and palm trees. You may enjoy the sunshine and tolerable air temperatures, but the fish are concerned with water temperatures. Consider also that cold fronts cross the state frequently, keeping weather patterns unstable and producing winds that can affect flats fishing.

Another thought worth remembering is that most of the leading guides are booked at least a year in advance for the prime months of tarpon fishing and during the peaks of the bonefish season. If you intend to fish at those times, you should make reservations early. An alternative is to fish the fringes of the season, such as late June or early July, when guides often have more time. There are still plenty of fish around and you can get to know your guide. If things work out, he may save an impressive time slot for you next year.

2 · Tackle, Equipment, and Boats

F LATS FISHING WILL PUT TACKLE TO THE TEST FASTER than any other phase of the sport. The fish are large and powerful and they have vast areas in which to run. The major fish of the flats will give you a pitched battle—and they won't give up.

Fish are lost through angler error or tackle failure. Concentration and technique can help improve the odds in the first instance, but there is virtually no excuse for tackle that does not measure up and is not maintained in prime condition. Underestimating the tenacity of one's quarry can be a costly mistake.

In the past decade, the advances in fishing tackle have been staggering. Today's anglers are not only better equipped than they were a few years ago, but they are far more knowledgeable and demanding. For those reasons, tackle is much lighter and more challenging than ever before.

Every piece of equipment is a compromise and should be viewed in that light. When dealing with species that roam the flats, one must set the dual objectives of presentation and doing battle. Tackle choices must reflect those requirements. The serious angler recognizes that opportunities on the flats can be gone forever in a matter of seconds. That is why it is so important to pick the right outfits and keep them in good working order.

SPINNING

Spinning is by far the most popular type of tackle in use today, because it affords flats fishermen quickness of presentation and ease of operation. Even when casting into the teeth of a stiff wind, there is practically no chance to tangle. Without thinking, one can cast a spinning rod forehand, off to the side, over the shoulder, or in any other direction. As a fighting tool, however, it has to be ranked third behind plug gear and fly tackle.

Regardless of the materials from which they are made, almost all spinning rods for use on the flats range from 6 feet to 7½ feet in length: most rods are 6½ feet or 7 feet long. There is no place for the very short, soft, ultra-light sticks that are often used in fresh water. A long rod casts farther with greater accuracy than a short one. Besides, you need a fighting tool with plenty of beef in the butt section.

When it becomes necessary to cast a live shrimp to a bonefish, some specialists use a cut-down fly rod blank that may be 8 feet or even 8½ feet in length. A comparison could be made to the steelhead rods used in Michigan and the Pacific Northwest, where it is necessary to present a very light bait and yet have enough backbone to fight the fish.

New materials constantly enter the rod-building arena. Not very long ago E-glass, or the first generation of fiberglass, was all we had. Then graphite came on the scene, along with various composites and boron. At the same time engineers went back to their drawing boards and developed a lighter and stronger fiberglass known as S-glass.

Each material offers specific advantages and disadvantages. The parameters for choosing a rod, however, remain the same regardless of the material from which it is made. When largemouth bass fishermen finally were shown the so-called "worm rod," which had a stiffer tip and more beef in the butt than previous models, they merely discovered what flats fishermen had been using for years.

To wrestle a fish effectively, you must be able to move its head and slug it out toe-to-toe in barroom-brawl fashion. In rod design, that translates into lifting power, or the reserve strength a rod blank has when you really apply the pressure. When you pull back on a rod, the resistance starts at the tip and moves progressively back to the butt. A soft tip merely collapses and so has a negative effect on performance. The greater the force applied, the faster and more completely it is transferred down the blank. Any part of the rod that points to the fish is not really contributing to fighting it.

When you choose a fighting tool, you must think in terms of this lifting power. Perhaps the day will come when rod manufacturers will show a measurement of lifting power for each blank. To establish some standard, we came up with a basic formula many years ago when working with the design of fly rods, but the principle is equally valid for all forms of tackle.

For battling big fish, a rod must be able to lift a five-pound weight off the floor with six inches of line extending beyond the tip top and still have some reserve power in the butt. Actually, there are times when you want the rod to lift more than that, but if you are going to tackle trophy tarpon and husky sharks on the flats, that becomes the minimum measurement. A bonefish rod should lift at least two pounds and possibly three pounds of weight off the ground with the same six inches of line extended. Using this data as a guide, you should be able to interpolate for the species you seek and the conditions under which you must fish.

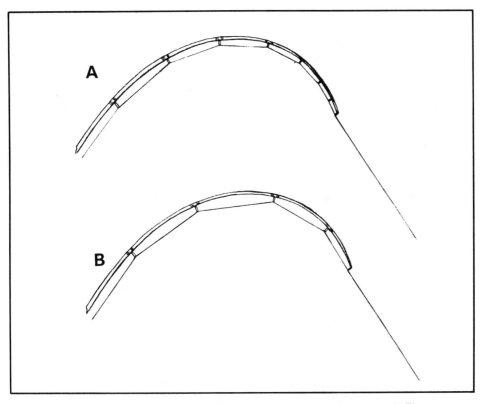

The line under pressure should follow the contour of the rod as shown in Figure
A—Figure B has too few guides.

Any rod you select should be able to cast the weight lures or bait you will
be using. The best advice anyone can offer is to try an outfit *before* you plunk
cash on the counter. When you are satisfied that the design and taper of the
blank will perform, your next step is to check the guides, guide placement,
reelseat, and the length and position of the grips.

String line through the guides and lock one end against the reelseat while
somebody maintains steady pressure on the other end. You are checking for
the right number of guides and their placement. The line, under pressure,
should follow the contour of the rod. Any sharp bends or radii show that there
are not enough guides or that they are placed wrong. Reject the rod. As a rule
of thumb, don't look at any rod that does not have at least five guides and a
tip top.

Line is going to be moving over those guides under pressure and with
incredible speed. Therefore, the guides must be top quality. Chrome over
stainless steel, aluminum oxide, and the various ceramics are usually good
choices. Tungsten carbide may be strong, but it will fray line quickly. It also
pits when used extensively in salt water.

If you have an opportunity to cast the rod, focus on the first guide, or the
gathering guide, as it is called. Its distance from the reel and its height above

the blank help to determine how well the rod will cast. We also like to see a gathering guide that is large enough for whatever size line you are using. If you observe the line slapping the rod or trying to force its way through this orifice when you cast, you know the size or placement is wrong.

Surprising as it may sound, the hoods on some reelseats will not accept all reel models. Sometimes there is not enough distance to fit the reelfoot, and at other times the height or thickness of the foot exceeds the tolerances of the hood. Whatever the problem, don't buy a rod that will not hold your reel.

Finally, look at the grips. To fight a fish, you want a reasonably short butt. It brings the reel in closer to your body so that you can keep your elbow in and locked against your side as you spin your wrist to turn the reel handle. If you have to reach well forward to find the reel handle, fatigue will begin sooner.

SPINNING REELS

Drag performance coupled with line capacity rank as the primary considerations in choosing a spinning reel. Any fish hooked in shallow water is going to make a long run. It is the only escape route. The fish cannot sound, so it has to dash for deep water. Hesitation in the drag system or inadequate line capacity will cost you a fish. There is no margin for error or failure.

As a minimum requirement, the reel you select should carry at least 200 yards of the line you plan to fish. In many situations, 250 to 300 yards would make more sense. Even if you follow your quarry with a boat, it takes time to get under way and you can be out of line before that happens.

Think of drag as resistance to rotation rather than as a brake. You do not want it to stop the spool, but merely to slow it down at a predetermined rate. It should perform smoothly at very slow speeds as well as when a fish has fired its afterburner and is streaking for the next county.

If possible, test the drag on a reel before you buy it. Put line on the spool and then go through the full range of drag settings. Whether the adjustment is on the spool or behind the housing, you want a reel that gives plenty of latitude for adjusting the drag. A reel that goes from barely any resistance to a locked drag in half a rotation of the adjustment knob is too critical. The more gradual the adjustment, the easier it is to obtain precise settings.

With the line around the bail and about 18 inches extending, set the drag so that the weight of the reel barely lowers it against the tension. This demonstrates slow-speed drag. If the reel seems jerky and drops erratically, it has drag problems.

Good drags alternate between hard and soft washers and use a spring-adjusted pressure plate to establish the setting. The spring is important because it helps to align the force and compensate for high and low spots. At the end of each day's fishing, the drag adjustment knob or starwheel should be loosened to relieve the pressure and allow the washers to return to their normal shape.

By pulling line off the reel sharply, you can get an inkling whether or not the drag binds in the starting position. As you crank it back on the spool, look to see that there is no build-up on one side of the spool or the other. Uneven reeling indicates that excess play in the line has not been adjusted through the addition or removal of shim washers.

Rollers and line guides constitute the third most important aspect of spinning reels. If they are properly designed, they will turn when line is pulled from the reel. A bushing under the roller usually improves things. Grease should be removed and light oil substituted under this part. Above all, it must be kept clean so that it will turn.

Most of the reels on the market feature skirted spools. They perform well and help to keep dirt from getting into the inner workings. Standard spool reels are smaller, easier to carry, cost less, and also do an excellent job. It's a matter of personal preference.

If you have an opportunity, take the sideplate off and look at the gears. They should be made from quality materials. Helical gears offer a faster

A preliminary check of any drag you're thinking of buying is to adjust it so the reel's weight will cause it to descend slowly. If it drops smoothly, the drag is probably a good one. If it falls in jerks, it will probably cause break-offs.

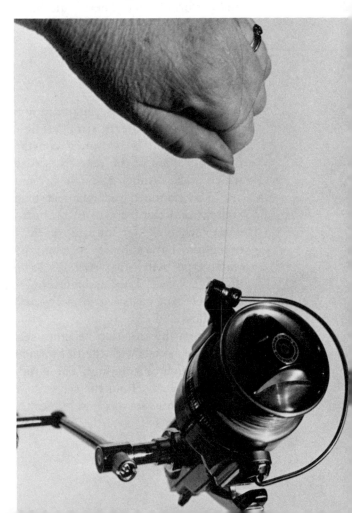

retrieve than straight ones. Most spinning reels now boast retrieve ratios of five-to-one or better. The increased retrieve makes sense because it allows you to work a lure faster and recover line with more speed. By using a shorter-handled arm with a standard reel, you can increase the speed of retrieve.

While you are studying the spinning reel, check the bail assembly. Those that can be opened and closed at will without the old-fashioned spring arrangements are a marked improvement. Internal trip is a quieter system for closing the bail, but external trip in which a projection on the spool strikes part of the reelstand works fine.

Reels in which the bail is opened by touching a single lever are now available, as are other innovations such as a silent anti-reverse or the ability to change the handle for right-handed or left-handed retrieve. Inspect a reel carefully and make certain it is manufactured from components that will resist corrosion. A tropical climate can be devastating on parts that are not protected.

Although most anglers use full-bail reels, a few still prefer the manual pickup in which the forefinger puts the line back slightly after the cast by catching it just before the lure strikes the water. The primary advantage of manual pickup lies in the absence of moving parts. Rollers are often larger and perform better. There is no bail to get out of shape or fail. Reels can be modified by installing manual rollers or, in some cases, by cutting the bail arm off the existing roller.

PLUG CASTING

In the right hands, plug-casting tackle—called baitcasting tackle in fresh water—proves to be the strongest fighting tool. It is a powerful weapon that is fun to use and is becoming constantly more popular among the angling fraternity. One of the reasons is casting-control improvements in the reels, which make it much easier to present a bait or lure without backlashing.

The standard rod is 7 feet long with the blank running through the reelseat and right down to the butt cap. A few models may be 6½ feet in length when lighter lines are used. Until recently, offset handles were the exception. Lately, however, a number of anglers have been using the fresh water type baitcasting rods for less rigorous assignments on the flats and doing very well. They are shorter (5½ or 6 feet), but they are comfortable to use where long casts are not necessary and where one does not have to battle a leviathan.

When the situation becomes serious in the shallows, veterans resort to the 7-foot models with the right amount of lifting power, as described earlier in the section on spinning. These rods have an exceptionally short butt—six to eight inches behind the reelseat—and the reelseat is often reversed, with the locking nuts forward, to reduce the actual distance to the reel. At first the concept seems awkward, but anyone who has entered the arena against

All of these reels work well on the flats and are capable of landing most species, with the exception of large sharks and tarpon. Usually, lines of 4- to 8-pound test are used on these modern, light-plug reels.

heavyweight competition quickly learns the value of being able to reach the reel and keep the rod close to the body. Sometimes, to cast with two hands, one must hold the butt as if it were a baseball bat.

There is a trend toward using lighter lines with plug gear. The six-pound-test line has already gained acceptance and a small group of dedicated fishermen are now trying four-pound-test line on plug. This necessitates lighter rods with slightly softer tips for casting small lures.

To select the right rod, follow the suggestions presented for the spinning enthusiast. A 7-foot plug rod with the blank reaching to the butt cap requires more guides than a spinning rod of the same length. Seven guides plus the tip top is a fair average. Be sure to run line through the guides and that the placement is correct so that the line follows the curvature of the blank.

Fishermen have never had a more varied choice of plug-casting reels than they do right now. Most of them are excellent. The first requirement is line capacity; those tailored for fresh water work generally do not hold enough line unless you drop way down in breaking strength. If you intend to take a 100-pound fish, you will need a reel that holds at least 225 yards of 15-pound-test line. Fifteen pounds has long been considered the standard on plug.

It is a small measure of pride rather than boastfulness that causes us to admit that we designed and were the primary forces behind the acceptance of the drag system used in most plug reels today. Along with Norman Jansik of Miami, Florida, who was the third member of our team, we researched the subject in the late 1960s and badgered manufacturers until they began to listen. We would be remiss if we did not share credit with the late Gordon Young of Miami, who contributed greatly to the project. Gordon's untimely passing left a double void in our lives; he was both a treasured friend and a trail-blazer who toiled diligently to improve fishing tackle for everyone.

After you have checked drag performance on a plug reel (and that is done in the same way as for spinning reels), try the handle. The knobs should be designed so that you can grab them easily and hold on for long periods of time. A short, sturdy handle makes it easier to spin so that you can increase the retrieve speed.

There are many specialists who prefer a line guide, or level wind, that moves back and forth during the cast, because the line then comes off the reel evenly instead of at an angle. This preference is being supressed by new designs that cast better when the line guide does not move.

At lower right is a conventional rod holder. Usually a rubber stretch cord is used to hold rods firmly on the small shelves. Inset shows how a small strip of Velcro is enclosed around the rubber stretch cord. Glued on the vertical part of the rod holder is the companion piece of Velcro. This allows the angler to pull only lightly on the rubber cord to hold rods and lock it with the Velcro.

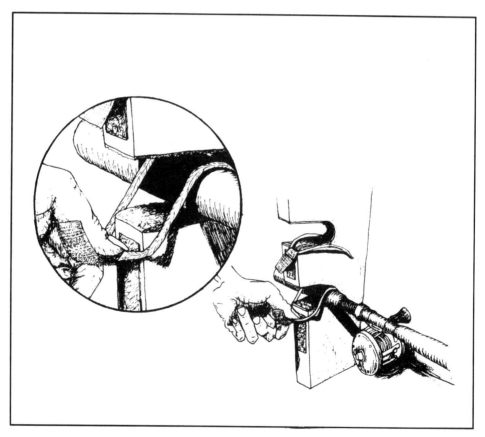

Plug casting reels that have centrifugal brakes that travel in a race inside the reel will occasionally build up dirt. The reel will seem to run smoothly, but distance is hampered. No problem—just clean the race and reassemble the reel.

It should be mentioned that spool shapes and magnetic casting controls offer new dimensions in sophistication. Before long, the average caster will handle plug tackle with almost as much ease as spinning tackle—and it's a lot more fun to use.

As a word of caution, reels with thumb bars that activate the free-spool button can cause problems. If you inadvertently touch it while fighting a fish, it is all over; you'll never get the backlash out.

For those who intend to use very light lines, make certain the tolerances between the spool flange and the sideplate are close enough so that the line does not slip through. Even with quick take-apart reels, which you should insist on, the line gets frayed back there and you will have to re-rig after cutting away the bad part.

FLY FISHING

The myth persists. Early writers on the subject insisted that the light-wand enthusiast had to use husky tackle in salt water. Rods that handle a 9-weight fly line were thought to be the minimum for bonefish and average work was performed with 10-weight or even 11-weight outfits. Wind, they concluded, was the culprit even if the fish weren't big.

Leading bonefish anglers are now resorting to trout tackle and rods that load properly with a 5-weight to a 7-weight line. If you are limited in tackle selection, you can certainly get by with two rods: an 8- or 9-weight and a 12- or 13-weight for almost all salt water fishing. The trend, however, is toward a more specialized approach just as it is in trout or salmon fishing.

Those who have made the transition from fresh water sport with a fly rod to salt water fly fishing have discovered that the marine version is equally challenging and that the person who can handle himself on the flats will become a better trout or salmon angler. There are differences to be mastered, but one fact summarizes the subject. In fresh water, the fish remains in nearly the same position for hours on end. You have ample time to change flies, reflect on the situation, or make any necessary adjustments. On the flats, the fish will be out of range or spooked almost before you can read this paragraph.

A fly rod must be able to transport the right fly over the required distance and to fight the fish effectively. There are refinements. Whether you are casting to a bluefish, pushing a fly back under the mangroves to a snook, or searching the water in a blind effort to locate striped bass, certain needs must be met. The key in these situations lies in longer casts with tighter loops and plenty of line speed. You want either to deliver the fly to the fish or to cover the largest possible area in the shortest amount of time. Longer casts allow a fish to follow before striking.

If you are trying to drop an offering in front of a tailing bonefish, a cruising permit, or a fussy mutton snapper, delicacy becomes critical. Merely unloading in the direction of the fish usually lights up the path to disaster. The fly must parachute to the water with a gentleness that allows it to fall reasonably close without alarming the fish.

A longer fly rod enables you to make better presentations in terms of both distance and delicacy. It also becomes vital if you have to lift a length of line off the water to cast a second or third time. A boron rod, by the way, lets you lift more line than a rod made from other materials because of its higher modulus of elasticity. With the newer materials, rods of 8½ feet to 9½ feet are perfect and a 9-footer is about the average. You also need this length if you are wading. There are times when a 10-foot rod might be an aid, but they are limited.

Regardless of the length of the rod you select or the type of fishing you intend to do with it, focus on the size of the guides. They must be large enough to allow the line to slip through easily and without any of the connections hanging for even an instant. The first guide or stripping guide should be

16mm in diameter. You probably will not find stripping guides that big because they don't look good, but it is worth having someone change it for you. Snake guides produce less friction than ceramic ones, but they wear faster. If you use snakes—and we like them on many of our rods—opt for the biggest ones made. Ceramic guides are an excellent choice for the stripping guide and the tip top. Whether or not you use them for all the guides is your decision.

When selecting a fly rod, the most important test is the recovery rate. You want a rod that dampens vibrations quickly and with a minimum of fluctuations. Hold the rod with the butt at your belt buckle and the blank parallel to the floor. Snap it sharply either vertically or horizontally and watch how many large and small vibrations occur. Each movement of the tip sends shock waves down the line and lowers casting speed and power. Compare a few rods and you will soon have an idea of the differences.

After that test, put the tip of the rod on the floor and grip the butt with one hand. Push forward and downward so that the rod starts to flex. Repeat the exercise and trace every inch with your eyes. If you see flat or dead spots, look for another rod.

With the rod at waist level, swing it back and forth slowly. You can actually see where the blank flexes. If it flexes near your hands, it is a slow-action rod. A fast-action design will flex in the tip section and a medium-action somewhere around the ferrule.

In most fishing, presentation plays the most significant role. However, if you are chasing the huskier denizens of the shallows, you also need a fish-fighting tool. Originally the theory was that if you somehow could get the fly to the fish, that was all you could expect from these meat-sticks. That concept is history. The newer rods not only have lifting power, but they are a pleasure to cast.

When graphite and the various composites were introduced, rod breakage was a factor in battling big fish. Problems occurred when one tried to lift with a rod that was extremely compressed at the bottom and maximally elongated at the top. Most of those design failures have been resolved and there are several graphite rods up to the task. Some anglers still prefer the newer S-glass and a few remain supporters of the traditional E-glass because it is more forgiving. This, of course, is a matter of choice.

Any fighting tool must have an extension butt to keep the reel away from your body. Our recommendation has always been a two-inch butt that is an integral part of the rod. A few tournaments impose this limitation, mainly because it is more effective than any other length. Butts that must be inserted are a problem, because you can never find them when you need them. Too long a butt will catch line when you are shooting on a cast.

It should be mentioned that serious fly fishermen usually have more than one rod rigged and ready. In the event of a break-off, they merely pick up another outfit and they are back in business. When things quiet down, they loop on another leader and make the first outfit operative. Having a number of rods also allows the fisherman to be ready for several different situations. You might be bonefishing, for example, but have one fly rod rigged for sharks and another for tarpon.

Quality fly reels have been a hallmark of the industry for a long time. Bob McChristian's Seamaster and the FinNor reels are standards. A number of other designs have also made their appearance and most are excellent. Fishing with one of these premier reels enhances the angling experience, but they are not essential to catching fish. The occasional practitioner or the person who merely wants to try the sport with a fly rod can find adequate tackle for less money. Some of the larger fresh water reels, for example, can have counterweights added to smooth their performance during staggering runs. As long as they have enough line capacity, they will work wherever drags are not really necessary.

A few fresh water reels do have respectable drag systems that will handle big fish. If you become addicted to fly fishing the flats, as we predict, you will eventually invest in at least one of the quality salt water reels.

Remember that the fly reel you select must hold both dacron backing and the fly line of your choice. The handle should be comfortable, and the reel should be streamlined so that line cannot hang or catch on any portion. It should, of course, be corrosion resistant.

Salt water has a destructive effect on tackle. There is a tendency to spray fresh water on a fly reel and feel that the cleaning task is done. You will discover, however, that without a mild detergent you cannot remove all the salt. At the end of a trip, we prefer not only to wash the reel in warm water and detergent, but also to put the line in a tub with warm water. To do this, you simply pull it off the reel. Then, as you crank it back on, wipe it with a sponge. In cleaning the reel, you will find that a toothbrush will help you to get into tight places, especially around the support pillars and recessed screwheads.

Given a choice of one fly line for flats fishing, the selection would have to be an intermediate line that sinks very, very slowly through the surface film. This is important in getting the fly to the fish and will help immeasureably on those days when dead grass floats on the water's surface. If, by the way, you tend to get grass on the fly, make a high forward roll cast followed by a violent backcast just before the hook comes out of the water. The surface tension of the water will cause the hook to cut through the weeds.

Although there are advantages to the intermediate line, most anglers use a floating line for working the tropical flats. One reason is that it is easier to pick up if you have to cast again. In either case, you should use a standard weight-forward fly line rather than a double taper, salt water taper, or level line. We'll have more to say about this in Chapter Six.

Those who fish large expanses of flats where water clarity is a problem and the activity involves blind casting often resort to shooting heads. We prefer to call them "search lines" because they enable one to make long casts. You can further increase your casting distance by making your own search line from a double-taper fly line. In casting generally, the line begins to fall as soon as the loop unfolds. The greater the length of line rolling out in a loop, the longer it takes to open and the farther it will go.

With this in mind, buy a double taper one size smaller than you are currently using on your rod. The standard shooting head is 30 feet, the size designation being based on the weight of that length. With a line one size smaller, you can make a 40-foot shooting head that weighs the same as the 30-foot head in the larger size. That extra length will improve your casting distance and you will find you can hold 40 feet of line in the air comfortably.

MONOFILAMENT LINE

Line has always been the weakest link in any tackle system. In a demanding situation such as fishing the flats, a compromise on line quality or condition has to be classified as false economy. Those who score consistently well in shallow water fishing are fanatics about line.

Start by buying a premium brand rather than bargain-basement mill ends that someone is trying to unload. All monofilament is not the same. There are no bargains. A premium line undergoes more steps in the manufacturing process and rigorous quality control.

If you are going to wage war with the bigger brutes, lines must be changed frequently. The same rule holds for bonefish, permit, and other denizens that run long distances. After each fish, be sure to check the line carefully, especially the tag-end around the terminal tackle.

The smaller the diameter of the line, the more natural a bait or lure will appear in the water. Fish can see all lines and leader material, but some blend in better than others. With a smaller diameter, the question is not whether they can see it, but what effect that diameter has on the action of the lure.

The color of the line can also make a difference. If you are in doubt, select a clear line. Look at it closely. Some lines labeled clear actually reflect light like a chandelier in the dining room. You want a non-reflective clear line. Advertisers often claim that certain fluorescent lines are totally visible to the angler above water, but that the fish cannot see them. That might make good copy in the ads, but if you go under water and look, as we have, you will know that the lines not only are visible, but they are much brighter than lines that are not fluorescent.

Monofilament is a very forgiving line because it has considerable stretch or elongation. This cushioning factor becomes evident when you start to put stress on the line. A typical monofilament may have 20 to 30 percent elongation built into the line. Once the stretch limit has been reached, the line itself starts to take the strain. If you relax the tension before you reach that point, the line returns to its original shape because the amount of stress was within the elastic limits.

Unless you break the line, there is no way to tell from looking at it when the elastic limits have been reached. However, once they are exceeded and even if the line does not break, it becomes permanently deformed and can no longer return to its original condition. That is why it may be important to change lines frequently in flats fishing. During the battle, assuming you have maximum pressure on the fish, you may weaken the line. If you do break off, the entire length from the reel to the tag-end has been stressed past the elastic limits and should be discarded.

Abrasion resistance of a line is another area of confusion. It has nothing to do with whether a line is hard or soft, limp or rigid. The property has to be built into the line. Researchers lately have been offering a number of laboratory tests to prove one point or another. Just keep in mind that you cannot measure abrasion resistance by running the line over sandpaper or in a dry environment. The line is fished underwater. Experience will soon teach you which lines perform best.

As a flats fisherman, you know that you will need accuracy of presentation, casting distance, and enough line to handle the long runs of the fish you will catch. These needs translate into reel spools that are filled to capacity. A spinning spool, for example, should be filled to within one-eighth inch of the lip. Plug reels are full when the line is up to the level of the spool flange, or just below it so you can remove the spool. Anything less than a full spool will cut down on your casting distance and accuracy, not to mention your ability to fight a fish.

BOATS FOR THE FLATS

Boats tailored for shallow-water fishing must draw a minimum of water both while underway and adrift. Possibly the best description we have ever heard was uttered by a Bahamian guide who insisted that his boat could go where water had been. That may be a slight exaggeration, but it is not far from the truth. The better flats boats can float in eight inches of water and some of them will just about bob in six inches.

Because they are poled, driven by an electric motor, or allowed to drift, this type of boat should have a minimum sail area. Most of those used in the Florida Keys, for example, have an extremely low profile and are characterized by incredible stability. Two men can walk down the same gunwale and the craft will barely lean in that direction.

Noise is a major factor on the flats, and a boat with sharp entry and without massive spray rails tends to be much quieter. A cathedral hull ranks

Care should be used in backing a car and trailer down a boat ramp. This steep one in Key West needs a block under the wheel. The driver didn't set the emergency brake—the car floated until a tow truck arrived to pull it out of the water.

Typical of the clean interior of a good flats boat is the Hewes Bonefisher, shown here. Note that the entire inside is lined with outdoor carpet, and there are no line-tangling cleats. Guide is placing pole in push-pole holder.

"X" marks the spot where the fly line lies on the deck. Note that the interior is clean and that the angler can make a good cast if he doesn't step on the line.

as about the worst design you can have from that standpoint, while lapstrake boats are quite good. Non-skid paint, floorboards, and outdoor carpeting can be used to deaden sound transmitted through the hull.

Center-console designs may work well in the offshore waters, but the steering station gets in the way on the flats. A small, unobtrusive console off to one side proves best. When light horsepower engines are used on aluminum skiffs or other small craft, steering is often accomplished with the aid of a tiller extension on the motor arm.

Elevation means everything on the flats as far as visibility is concerned. Platforms help to keep anglers isolated and up high where they can see. They are also designed to hold fly lines off the cockpit floor where they might tangle. For the fly fisherman, there is a much better solution. If you have your own boat, why not create two platforms with the forward one slightly higher than the one that abuts it. That way, you can fish from the upper one and use the lower platform for the fly line. A retaining lip will prevent the fly line from falling to the deck.

Most guides have constructed a poling platform over the outboard in the stern of their boats. This not only allows them to pole the boat on the centerline, but it gives them valuable elevation above the water. One suggestion here is to construct a tiny lip around the edge of the platform so that it can be felt by the foot and the poler will know when he's on the edge.

Typical flats scene from a top guide's boat. Pole has been stored properly in holders. Angler is standing on bow looking for bonefish, motor has been lifted, in case a hooked fish runs under the boat and possibly cuts the line on the motor, and the anchor line has small release anchor buoy on line.

The fiberglass pushpole has been the standard means of propulsion for years. It is silent and one can position a boat beautifully with it. Without a high poling platform, bonefishermen can get by with a 14-foot pole because the water is relatively shallow. With the platform, an 18-foot pole becomes necessary. Tarpon are found in deeper waters and most serious fishermen use electric motors to chase these fish. As a guideline, figure one to one and a half pounds of thrust for every hundred pounds of gross boat weight, which includes everything and everyone on board. Chances are you will need an electric motor with at least 25 pounds of thrust. Be sure to get one with two or three forward speeds.

A boat becomes a very private and personal choice. Not everyone likes the same thing.

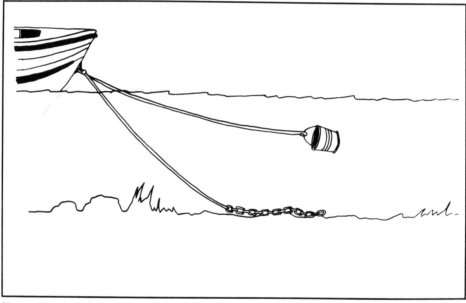

There are times when you want to drift a basin or deeper stretch, but want to control the speed of the drift. You can drag a heavy chain on a rope along the bottom, as shown, or stream a bucket on a rope as a sea anchor behind the boat. This also prevents the boat from spinning slowly on the drift.

3 · Understanding Tides

Tides play a greater and more significant role in shallow-water fishing than in any other type. They determine where the fish will be and when they will be there. Without an understanding of this subject, no angler can consistently catch fish on the flats. For the fresh water aficionado, tides are a new concept and a difficult one to fathom. Even the deep-water marine angler has problems wrestling with tidal factors when dealing with only a foot or two of water.

Just off Seven Mile Bridge on the magnificent Overseas Highway that travels through the Florida Keys, two pretty flats are separated by a channel no wider than a football field. From the roadway both shallow areas look alike and, even with the advantage of height, one can detect no differences. The fish do, however. One of those flats may be extremely productive during incoming tide. You won't find a fish on the other until the tide turns and starts to fall. And when that happens, the first flat becomes totally void of fish.

Throughout the tidal stages, a labyrinth of currents, eddies, and miniature upwellings are created across the flats as the moving water follows the irregular contours of the bottom and strikes every mound and rise. Anyone who has fished a stream or river already knows how currents can affect their quarry. It is no different on a flat, except that the current is also adjusting the overall amount of water as well as its depth.

THE CAUSE

Although there are a few places in the world that have only one low and one high tide daily, known as diurnal tides, most are characterized by two high tides and two low tides daily, approximately six hours apart and known as semidiurnal tides. Since the moon to a large degree and the sun to a lesser degree affect the tides, their relative positions are important.

When the sun and moon are in direct alignment with the earth, the gravitational forces are strongest. This alignment occurs during the new moon—that is, when the moon is not visible in the sky—and when the moon is full, and causes the high tides to be higher than average and the low tides lower. These are called *spring tides*, although they have no relation to the season of the year. When the moon is positioned at right angles to the alignment of the earth and the sun, the moon is either at first quarter or third quarter. Gravitational pull drops to a minimum and the tidal range falls below average. Tides under these conditions are called *neap tides*.

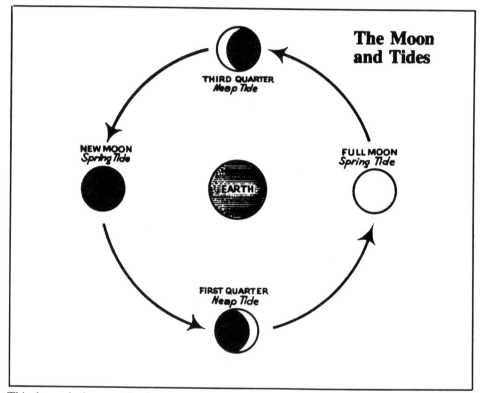

This shows the lunar cycle of one month. At quarter moons the angler knows that he will experience neap tides; at the new and the full moon tides will be extra high and extra low—spring tides will be occurring.

The lunar day during which tides occur spans 24 hours and 50 minutes. As a result each tidal stage will be 50 minutes later tomorrow than it is today. If you found fish on a particular flat this morning at ten o'clock, they should be there tomorrow shortly before eleven.

Tides rotate on a two-week cycle, so that fishing conditions should be the same on the flat we just discussed two weeks from today at ten o'clock as they are today. They will be just the opposite one week from today. If the tide is high at noon today, it will be dead low at the same time one week hence.

Simply by looking at the moon, you can tell instantly if you are in a period of spring tides or neap tides. Keep in mind that even though there are generally two low tides and two high tides daily, one high tide will put more water on the flats than the other and one of the low tides will be lower. The amount is shown in a Government publication entitled "Tide Tables for the East Coast of North and South America." There is a companion publication for the West Coast and they are available in most marine supply shops and some fishing tackle stores.

The appendices of this book give the tides for major points along the coast along with a series of tables with correction factors that can be added to or subtracted from the base data to figure tides at many other locations. Once you know the tide differences for an area you want to fish, you can make the needed calculations quickly.

Wind and barometric pressure also affect the tides and the tidal range. During periods of high atmospheric pressure, slightly less water fills a flat than it would if the pressure were low. Wind speed, direction, duration, and fetch—the distance over which the wind blows—can all have an effect on the amount of water on a flat. When the wind blows in the same direction as the outgoing tide, the low will be lower because the wind is helping to get the water off the flat. However, the high will also be lower, because the same wind tends to hold back the incoming water. Tides pile up and more water floods the flats when a strong wind pushes the rising tide. The same wind direction will slow the ebb tide and push water back into the flat. These conditions affect various flats differently and it takes local knowledge to know just what will happen. It is, however, important data to collect and remember.

THE EFFECT

Before you can catch fish on the flats, you have to find them. You already know that some spots harbor fish on incoming water, while others produce on outgoing. This is basic, but it is also an oversimplification. Fish might show, for example, on the last couple of hours of a tide or right at the beginning. If a flat looks as if it will hold fish, you have to check it out during the various stages and during neap tides as well as spring tides. Only then will you begin to see a pattern. When you have mastered these clues, consider that guides talk about flats that should be fished at one season of the year or another.

Each area must be evaluated independently. Think about the specific effect of a spring tide. Since at that time there will be more water on a flat during the six-hour period leading up to high tide, fish should start to come up sooner and push up farther on the flat than they might have during a neap tide. In some places, fish will go to the end of a shallow channel during neap tides and hold in the pocket or along the edge of the deeper flats. Spring tides may create enough water to allow the fish to get to the top of a flat and scatter.

More water means that the fringes of mangrove-lined islands will fill and the fish can swim back under the limbs, making themselves inaccessible to the angler. All of these facets should be reviewed.

A lot more water has to empty off a flat during a spring low tide. The movement creates a strong flow, which translates into the fact that the fish may leave earlier and drop farther back. They are also much more skittish when they know that the water is falling fast. The strong ebb of the tide should serve as a warning to you as well. More than one skipper has found his craft aground. It happens so quickly on some flats, that if you begin to get caught, there is no way you can pull the boat off fast enough—and that includes jumping into the water to do it.

When you study a flat, try to relate the depth of the water and the other tidal conditions to the species of fish you intend to catch. There are times when bonefish, redfish, tarpon, and sharks will prowl with their backs out of water. It is not uncommon to see bonefish trading back and forth in very shallow water, waiting for the gentle surge of the incoming tide and following it right across the flat.

Exceptions are the fun part of flats fishing. Take nothing for granted and you will be ahead of the game. During the early summer, tarpon feed in one area of Florida Bay with half their bodies out of the water. A scant five miles away, you will never find those fish in less than three and a half or four feet of water.

When you are bonefishing in one foot to eighteen inches of water, it pays to be alert for tailing fish. You know as the water gets deeper that you won't see a tail unless it is truly a trophy fish. When water depth exceeds three feet, finding bonefish becomes difficult. It is not that they aren't there, but they are tough to spot and tougher to fish.

In a trout stream bait lives in one area, darting in and out of cover. On the flats, it doesn't work that way. Most bait fish do not have a permanent home and never attempt to stay in one place. For that reason, bait does not try to fight the tide, but merely goes along with it. Predators know this and use the tide to their advantage.

Snook may lie along the oyster bars in wait for tiny creeks and channels to drain. The bait stay in these spots for protection until the bottom of the tide, when the last of the water runs out. That is the best stage to fish this habitat.

On the other hand, bait fish also stay in very shallow water and work up the flat with the incoming tide, hoping to be in water too thin for game fish to reach them. The interesting part of all these strategies is that the predators know where the food supply will be. If you focus on these facts, you will have an idea of where to fish.

The variations over very short distances in the occurence of tides and the amount of water displaced may be significant when you are dealing with flats. This is particularly true in places like the Florida Keys, the Bahamas, or other tropical locations with extensive systems of shallow water. In many instances, you may have to do your own calculations to figure the times of the tides. Once you do, relate them simply as time differences from areas where you know the tides, or match them to places you fish regularly.

The shape of a flat, along with the size of the major body of water that feeds it and its proximity to this water, helps to determine when to fish it. Flats that drop off into an ocean, gulf, or major body of water tend to be better on incoming tide. The fish follow the flood of water on the flats and move to shallower and shallower water as the stage reaches high tide. If there is a plateau or shallow top to the flat, you can look for fish at the high water mark. There is also a chance they will continue down the other side and into a bay or estuary.

Think about the whole area and its tidal patterns. Where would the fish hold and where are they coming from? They may not be able to get to a certain flat early in the tide even though the water is deep enough, because they have to cross places that are inaccessible until later in the tide.

Tide direction can have an impact on the fish species you seek. Tarpon tend to go with the tide or across it, allowing the flow of water to push them forward or shoulder them up against a shallow bank where they are likely to find food. They have a tendency to follow these edges, moving in and out with the contour. That is why it is often possible to stake out the boat and wait for these fish to come to you along the known routes.

Newcomers to tropical flats frequently stare in amazement when a guide accurately predicts where and when they will see fish. These anglers suddenly see their mentor as a wizard with a crystal ball. Instead, experience demonstrates that the fish follow certain patterns and should be at a precise spot when the tide is at a specific height. He also knows that species such as tarpon or bonefish will take the same route daily, because that is the way the flow of water directs them and the bait.

Bonefish, permit, and redfish swim into the tidal flow because they use their sense of smell to locate food. It is surprising how far away they can detect the aroma of something good to eat, before they ferret it out of the bottom. The stronger the current, the better they feed.

Given a choice, most experienced anglers will pick a period of spring tides for flats fishing. There are exceptions, of course, but generally the more extreme changes produce better fishing. If you are planning a trip or want to book a guide, check the tide tables first. Those days with the greatest tidal differences between high and low water should be the best. Even without the tables, if you choose a time when a new or full moon will occur, you are in the right period. Quarter moons produce poorer fishing as a rule.

Tides and water temperature, when matched to a particular species, offer important clues to when and where fish will be. There are countless other factors, however, that no one really understands. People may try to give reasons, but they are only guessing. Experienced anglers find fish because

Use a pencil to mark charts, or a permanent pen. Most ball-point and regular felt-tips have water soluble inks, and you will lose your markings if the chart gets wet.

they play the percentages and because they use their local knowledge and observations.

If you fish an area regularly, keep a log of tide changes, date, weather, time of year, and what you saw or caught. It is much easier to detect a pattern when poring over notes than to construct one mentally. Guides are always on the lookout for new areas and unusual occurrences. Sometimes when they go from one spot to another, they take an unfamiliar route, scouting the flats along the way.

One can be reasonably certain that the fish will appear in the same places under similar conditions. They are creatures of habit and pattern. Knowing where and when they will show takes a great deal of experimentation and knowledge. That is why it is particularly difficult for an angler who has just arrived in flats country from some other part of the world to fish successfully.

Without an understanding of tides, tidal conditions, and their effects on various flats, there simply isn't enough time for the initiate to isolate the best fishing without being plain lucky. A guide is a good investment, at least for the first couple of days.

Local tackle merchants are often willing to share information about fishing spots. If they suggest places for you to fish, be sure to ask them what stage of the tide is best and when it occurs in those locations. If you do not know the precise time of the tide, you may wait a long time for the right conditions.

Anglers sometimes make the assumption that the tide rises and falls at a uniform rate throughout the six-hour period. That's not necessarily true. Remember that you have slack water at the top of the tide and again at the bottom. Then, the flood or ebb begins. Generally one short period, such as the middle two hours, accounts for 50 percent of the water exchange, with the rest occurring in the first and last two-hour segments. You sometimes find flats where nothing seems to happen for the first three hours of an outgoing tide, after which the water pours off as if someone has opened the flood gates.

Tides hold the key to shallow water fishing. When you learn about them, the door to superb fishing will swing open for you.

4 · Spotting Fish

THERE IS A DIFFERENCE BETWEEN LOOKING AND SEE-
ing. Most of us walk around with our eyes wide open, yet we fail to really see
everything unless we send a command to our brain to focus on it. If you had
walked into a room for the first time, you would be hard-pressed to recall
what you saw without having made a specific effort to note each individual
item in the room. On the flats, we must do precisely that. We must train
ourselves to spot fish as well as learn to recognize the signs.

In northern latitudes where even the shallow water lacks transparency,
most of the fishing is done with long, search-type casts. An alert angler may
detect a swirl on the surface as a bluefish or striped bass pounces on prey or
glimpse some other telltale sign. Basically, however, casting and retrieving
become somewhat mechanical. Those who take the sport seriously will watch
their lures, hoping to catch sight of a fish following. Beyond that, the method
is known as blind casting because you do not see a specific fish before making
the presentation.

On the tropical flats, the techique takes a totally different form. Instead
of casting, you stand alert with your rod at the ready, scanning the water until
you see a specific fish. Fly, lure, or bait must then be cast ahead of and beyond
your quarry. Hundreds of fish may be cruising the flat, but until you are able
to spot them, nothing happens.

POLARIZED SUNGLASSES

There is no alternative. Without polarized sunglasses, you will not be
able to see fish underwater. Polarization cuts through the surface glare and
reflections, making it possible to look into the water and focus on the bottom.

The darkness or lightness of the lenses has little to do with the protection
of your eyes in extremely bright light. Instead, you must determine the light-
absorbtion quality of the lens. Good glasses will absorb from 75 to 90 percent
of the ambient light.

Polarized sunglasses are currently available in a number of colors and materials. Though plastic is the least expensive, whether it is made into full-frame glasses or clip-ons for those who already wear glasses, it scratches easily. The best glasses available today feature a polarizing filter sandwiched between two pieces of glass. It is also possible to buy these with your prescription ground in and some houses even offer bifocals.

If you must choose one color for the flats, it should be brown. A brownish tint enhances contrast and makes it easier to see fish under typical flats conditions. Sometimes, the brown is really a combination of brown and gray or brown and green. The latest entries in the field tend to blend the basic colors with gray, blue, or green, creating more sophisticated lenses.

Serious fishermen recognize that a single pair of polarized sunglasses will not give optimum performance in every situation, so they carry at least two or three pairs of different colors and densities. An excellent solution to this problem lies in photochromatic polarized glasses. They lighten or darken depending on outside conditions, yet they filter out most of the ambient light. Currently, photochromatics are available in several colors including yellow.

A hat with a wide brim and polarized sunglasses are standard equipment for the serious flats angler. Without them, one is at a serious disadvantage.

Yellow, by the way, is the perfect choice for very early or late in the day and under overcast conditions. It tends to build contrast. Once you use them, you will be amazed. One alternative is to use yellow Kalichrome lenses with a polarized clip-on over them during full daylight. When the light levels fall, use yellow alone.

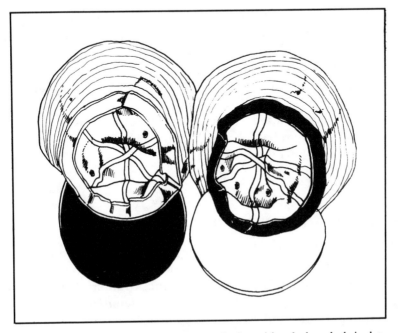

You can see much better with a hat on, and a hat with a dark underbrim lets you see even better. A simple method of darkening a hat without a dark underbrim is to paint it with black liquid shoe polish; let it air a day before wearing.

In order to see fish, you must build a tent around your eyes. That means that the glasses must wrap around the face or side-shields should be attached. Side-shields can be cut from inexpensive plastic polarized sunglasses or clip-ons and attached in several ways. You can glue trimmed pieces to each temple bar or they can be drilled and secured with tiny screws available from any shop that deals in eyeglasses. Pop rivets can also be used.

A broad-brimmed hat is just as essential as glasses. The one you select should have a dark color under the brim. In an emergency, you can use a felt-tip marker or black liquid shoe polish to darken the underside, but it is a lot easier to buy a hat with the color already there. When the hat is pulled down, it should fit securely over the top of the glasses, preventing light from filtering into your eyes along your forehead.

In the heat of battle, sunglasses have a way of falling into the water. People also have trouble remembering where they packed those glasses. The solution to both of these problems is to drill angled holes in the end of the temple bars and insert monofilament. The mono is knotted so it cannot come out. The knots must be on the outside of the temple bars to avoid irritating your skin. Measure the length of the mono. With the glasses in place, you should just be able to slip two fingers between the monofilament and the back of your head.

Another method is to wrap the mono tightly around a length of wire coat hanger and put it in hot water. When you pull it out, dip it in cold water and it will have tight coils just like the cord on your telephone receiver. It will then keep the glasses in place and from sliding off your nose, and you won't have loose mono dangling behind your head. When you take the glasses off, it expands.

Whenever you go on the flats, you should carry at least one spare pair of polarized glasses and probably more. Without them, you risk damage to your eyes and you won't be able to see fish.

SCANNING THE WATER

The quality of one's vision is not nearly as important in flats fishing as knowing how to look and recognizing the signs. If there is a secret other than experience and practice, it lies in total concentration. This is not casual fishing where you can let both the eyes and mind wander aimlessly. It demands a determined and systematic approach.

Every inch of height above the water increases the chances of seeing fish. That is the primary reason guides now use poling platforms over their engines. If the gunwale is a few inches above the casting platform in the bow and there is room to stand on it, that is where you belong. Don't discount those few inches.

Whenever possible, you want to have the sun at your back. The glare from puffy, white clouds is an added hindrance to visibility; if it gets too bad, you may have to angle the boat. The important point is to move to a position where you can see. Under certain circumstances, you may want to keep the boat very shallow, which allows you to scan the deeper water. The reverse may be true. Just remember to position and work the boat so that you can see.

Think of your head and eyes as a radar antenna. You want a fish to break the "beam." The trick is to look at the bottom. Don't be distracted by surface reflections or anything in between. When you are concentrating on the bottom, you will instantly detect anything that moves above it. Start your search pattern close to the boat and work farther and farther out until you are at the limits of your vision. Then, bring your eyes back to the first spot and start over again.

A platform over the motor allows the poler to see fish even before the angler, and increases visibility.

Beginners have the habit of allowing their gaze to remain in one spot, or they search at random without establishing a pattern. Occasionally, look back and check the area right around the boat. It is surprising how often a big fish will suddenly appear after eluding the radar approach you have been using.

As you scan, be alert to any type of movement. That is not always easy, because if the boat is being poled, it often seems as if everything is in motion. With experience, you'll begin to distinguish things that are moving at different rates from the boat. Some species such as barracuda and, at times, tarpon, may be lying perfectly motionless. Seeing them is not always easy, but that is where concentration comes into play. You have to keep telling yourself what you are seeing and questioning anything you are not certain about.

Polarization does not work at every angle. A useful trick is to tilt your head when you are having difficulty identifying something. This often helps by changing the polarization. Once you do make a positive identification and are sure it is a fish, you have the option of casting or ignoring it. Let's assume that what you saw was a small barracuda and you are after bonefish. When you know that object over there is a 'cuda, forget about it and continue your scan. If you keep watching it, you could miss a school of bonefish.

Knowing your quarry helps. When the water is less than a foot deep, almost all game fish will create a surface wake as they move. This wake may be almost imperceptible if the fish is going slowly, but it is there. For that reason, in very shallow water, you may want to spend most of your time looking across the surface rather than at the bottom.

Regardless of water depth, you should periodically lift your head and scout the surface at long distances. What you see may be surprising. There may be a commotion or a telltale fin or even a wake to alert you. The point to remember is that you have to look at every inch of water both beneath the surface and above it.

RECOGNIZING THE SIGNS

Hunters learn early in the game that they do not always see the entire animal standing out clearly. A deer hunter, for example, may only see a patch of white on the tail or the tines of the antlers. It is no different on the flats. You may see part of a fish or glean some indication that fish are there. Recognizing these signs is vital.

Many of the flats species have silver sides, almost like mirrors that tend to reflect the bottom. Over white sand they may appear as dark shadows, but when they swim over turtle grass, they are much more difficult to detect because the shadows are not very pronounced. A flats fisherman often will have at least one story about a fish six feet long that escaped his gaze until it suddenly appeared right alongside the boat.

Bonefish usually move into the tide and they seldom stop swimming. There are odd occasions when a bonefish might be "laid up," but you can almost always count on them to be underway. A stationary fish is probably a barracuda. If the water is very shallow, you might see tailing bonefish. As they dip their noses down to pick a tidbit off the bottom, their tails extend above the surface of the water. Frequently, they will glint silver in the sun and wave like so many flags. It is a treasured sight and one that a flats fisherman never forgets.

If the water is exceptionally shallow, you may see a bonefish swimming with its tail and dorsal extending above the surface. Single fish and schools tend to push water when they move in skinny surroundings and these wakes are easy to spot. Keep in mind that any wake streams off the fish from behind the dorsal fin. Newcomers want to cast just in front of the wake and the offering often lands on the head of the fish. Remind yourself that the head of a single fish or the lead fish in a school is well in front of that V that stretches behind it.

As a bonefish picks up food, it often blows water through its gills. This creates small patches of roiled water known as *muds* to the bonefishing fraternity. They dissipate quickly as the tide sweeps through them. With experience, you can detect even minor turbidity. When you do see muds, look around for the freshest ones, which will be darkest in color. That's where the fish are or the area they just left. In some Caribbean areas, bonefish schools are so large that they create massive muds while feeding. Check out the coloration and work the part that seems darkest.

On windy days when visibility is poor, you can sometimes spot cross ripples made by a school of bonefish. To do this, you have to be conscious of the direction of the pattern that the wind prints on the surface. Anything that moves counter to that pattern represents fish swimming beneath the surface. It may seem like grasping at straws, but experienced guides will amaze you with their ability to spot cross ripples.

Redfish exhibit many of the signs associated with bonefish. You won't find them on the same flats, but the signals may be similar. Look for tailing and mudding reds. They also create wakes when they swim in thin water and may move with dorsal fin and tail above the surface.

Rays may not be your target, but their presence on the flats is usually a good indication that other species are there. They are bottom feeders and use their wings to disturb the bottom, creating impressive muds in the marl or sand. The mud from a ray is usually larger and more pronounced than that made by bonefish, redfish, or permit. Rays also leave a surface wake behind them when they are in shallow water. It is tough to tell the difference between wakes and each one should be checked out until the fish that made it has been positively identified.

Several species, including jacks, permit, bonefish, redfish, and mutton snapper, sometimes follow rays, darting out to grab any escaping goodie frightened by the bigger fish. Even if you can identify the ray, cast behind it or at least look behind it for signs of other fish.

Permit can be extremely difficult to spot. One reason is that they prefer the deeper waters where visibility isn't as good. At times, you can see them tailing and the sickle tail with its black outline stands out sharply. Permit also have the habit of laying up on the surface with their dorsals and tails extending above the waterline. These may look like a couple of twigs puncturing the surface or you may just see a bit of black. Chances are that you will not spot the entire outline of the fish at first glance. Knowing the signs will help you here.

Barracuda have dark backs and invariably lie motionless in ambush for their prey. They have been described as looking like logs in the water. These fish do have a distinct way of swimming and if they are in motion, you can identify them by their undulations. That takes a bit of experience, but it will become routine after awhile.

The dorsal fin of the shark has been legendary throughout history. It is common on the flats to see the distinctive dorsal cutting through the water. Very often, you will notice the tail as well. Because the shark has a skeleton made of cartilage, it moves through the water with a back-and-forth swimming motion. Even at a distance, sharks look brown or black in the water and this is one way to identify them.

Lying at the edge of a sand patch, a snook may resemble a barracuda. Unless the angle is right and you can see the shape or the pronounced lateral line of the snook, it is difficult to tell the difference. When snook hit prey near the surface, they "pop" the water with their tails. The sound approaches the report of a rifle and once you've heard it, it's easy to identify. If you look in the direction of the noise, you will sometimes see bubbles on the surface marking the spot where the strike took place.

Nothing in flats fishing is more distinctive than the roll of a tarpon. These fish have an inferior lung arrangement and they come up to the surface from time to time to gulp air. As they do, their backs clear the surface and you can spot their silver sides. Rolls take different configurations, but all of them are highly visible. Sometimes right after a roll you will see air bubbles rise to the surface caused by the fish releasing some of the air it just gulped.

Mullet are an important part of a tarpon's diet and the silver kings will charge into a school of bait fish, exploding them in all directions. Just as easily, a tarpon may lie on the bottom totally motionless, or it may lay up near the surface with the tip of the dorsal and tail exposed. These are tough fish to see and you can be almost on top of them before you detect their presence.

On the northern flats where bluefish prowl, the primary forage is menhaden. These are oily fish and when bluefish chop them up in a feeding frenzy a slick develops across the surface of the water. Slicks can be seen—and smelled—at a considerable distance. If you watch closely, you can also identify bluefish breaking the water as they feed. These breaking fish are in the feeding mode and usually receptive to almost anything tossed in their path.

In slightly deeper water over the flats, a school of fish often creates a condition known as *nervous water*. It appears as if the surface is shimmering or vibrating. Once you learn to recognize this phenomenon, it will attract your attention and you will take the time to check out its cause.

Any fish up on the flats is skittish. When more than one fish is present, the entire body will react to the motions of a single school member. That means that if you spook one fish, all of them are gone. When you sight a fish or several fish and are ready to cast, take a precious moment to scout the fringes. You are looking for additional fish that might be frightened if the line goes across them or the lure falls too close.

Spotting fish is a learned technique and it takes practice. Each day you are on the water, you will get better at it. Remember that guides are familiar with the flats they fish daily. If you were to take them to new territory, even they would have to spend a little time adjusting. As the saying goes, "Seeing fish requires practice, practice, practice!"

5 · Finding Fish

No MATTER HOW GOOD AN ANGLER ONE MAY BE IN northern waters, conditions and techniques are so radically different on the tropical flats that, without a guide, failure is likely. Exploring on your own offers an exciting challenge and a fun way to fish, but it really should not be attempted until you see first-hand how a professional goes about it.

The overall budget of the trip should include the cost of a guide, at least on the first day and possibly the second. He can show you very quickly how to spot fish and the signs for which you should look. You will also get an idea of how he works a flat and the importance of tidal stages. Note how he tends to hang in an area for a while even though he doesn't see fish immediately. Experience tells him the fish are there and he seeks them out. If he is wrong, he moves on to the next spot or changes locations depending on what the tide is doing. If it's windy, he knows where to find a lee.

The majority of guides recognize that you are seeking information and most will help you. You can check this out before you hire a particular skipper by asking for references or by putting the question directly to him. Be certain he is experienced in the type of fishing you want to do. It does not make sense to book a guide for fly fishing when he prefers spinning. While you have him on the phone, ask about the species that are available during the time of year you plan to fish. If he levels with you, you won't be disappointed.

WADING

The goal, of course, is to find fish on your own. You can wade for bonefish, but permit and tarpon frequent flats that are too deep to walk on. If you are going to wade, the best advice is to stop in a couple of tackle shops and ask the people where they would recommend you fish and the stage of the tide that is best for each area. They will gladly share this information with you.

Newcomers to wading insist on trying to cover a great amount of terrain in the shortest possible time. A better approach is to move slowly and look for the signals that spell fish. You may see tails, wakes, cross ripples, nervous water, or something else that attracts your attention. Above all, you must see the fish and when you are wading, you lose the advantage of height. Therefore the fish are often much closer to you when you spot them. That is a perfect reason to move slowly and quietly.

Never wade without shoes. The spiny sea urchin makes a home on the flats and, if you step on one, will inflict a painful wound. At the same time, rays sometimes bury themselves in the bottom. Step on one and the barbed tail may cause a problem. Waders must learn to shuffle their feet so that they move a ray out in front of them instead of stepping on it.

Fish use the tide to their advantage. If they climb on a flat with rising water, they will work higher and higher as the tide continues to flood. When the tide is falling, they drop back with the receding water. That means you must look in both shallow and deep water, tracing a zigzag pattern until you find the fish. We once recommended a flat to someone who wanted to catch bonefish. Not only was he unable to spot fish, but he worked the wrong part of the flat, remaining deep while the fish were shallow. He later told us disappointedly that he had not seen a fish. Another angler on the same flat noted that he had seen several hundred fish.

Wading offers an economical approach to bonefishing. It also harbors an extra measure of sport, because you stalk the fish on foot. Besides, it affords the perfect opportunity to really study a flat and observe the intricacies of life on it.

APPROACHING A FLAT

If you have trailed your own skiff or have access to one, the flats are your domain. It goes without saying that the boat you use should draw very little water, and you should be able to guide its course with a pushpole, electric motor, or both. A pole, by the way, can be made quickly if you do not have one. Go to a lumber yard and buy a long piece of closet dowling. Try the different diameters until you find one that is comfortable in your hand. Get two small blocks of wood and secure them to one end of the closet pole with nails or screws. You are in business. The best poles, of course, are made from fiberglass and have aluminum fittings at either end.

More shallow-water fishing is ruined because of an improper approach than for all other reasons combined. Silence is the golden rule if you intend to be successful in shallow water. Enter a flat noisily and there is an excellent chance that you will never see a fish. Outboard-motor noise can frighten fish, and you can bet that sounds transmitted through the hull of the boat will have the same effect. Even a pushpole banging on hard rock can cause vibrations that alert your quarry.

Experienced guides learn where the fish will be and choose a point some distance away to ease onto the flat. They then pole from there to the fish. It is not that guides enjoy poling. Pushing a boat is hard work, but it is the most effective way to approach the fish silently. You could get upwind or upcurrent and drift, but that deprives you of a specific route and provides only random direction.

Why not use an outboard? Here's one example of its effect. We had poled a considerable distance to some tarpon that were laying up in very shallow water. Once in position, we selected a fly rod and began to make our presentations. The fish never moved. At that precise moment, someone cranked an outboard at least a quarter of a mile away and possibly farther. Without hesitation, the tarpon started to swim away. They were not panicked because of the distance, but they were alarmed and decided to ease out of there. Noise can have that effect.

Some years ago, we fished one area out of Key West regularly and knew where the fish should be. At first, we motored up to within 100 yards and poled the rest of the way. We saw very few fish until we realized that we should have poled about three times that distance. Once we changed our habits, the fishing was fantastic.

Knowledge of the flats you fish is paramount. The best way to learn any area is to view it at dead-low water on the lowest spring tides you can find. Every obstruction and shallow spot will be visible. Parts of the flat may be out of the water and you can study them carefully. The channels that lace through the flat and the deeper areas are showing clearly and you will have no doubt where they are. Take out a pencil and paper and make a map or put notes on the chart of the area so that you can recognize these features even when the tide is high and they are not showing.

You already know that you should fish a flat during spring tides because there is a greater flow of water with more extreme highs and lows. Fish like these conditions and are often more active when they exist. Having done low-water scouting, you may have to come back at high water to catch fish, but at least you will know the layout.

Constantly changing engine speeds draw the worst reaction from fish. The outboard should be throttled down from high speed some distance from the flat. If you are motoring for any distance, do it at low r.p.m. and without changing the throttle setting. A lot depends on where you fish. Flats bordered by heavily traveled channels tend to hold fish that have built up a tolerance to motor noise. On the other hand, there are backcountry flats that will be barren of fish for hours and even days if too many boats run over them.

Once you are in the fishing area, care must be taken to avoid making noises that will be transmitted through the hull. Someone opens a hatch, for example, and lets it drop with a sharp report. A tackle box is dragged and scraped along the deck. The angler jumps off the casting platform and lands on deck with a thud. An anchor is unceremoniously tossed over the side so that it makes a massive splash. All these and other noises may spoil the fishing. Fish are that sensitive.

Everyone knows that fish cannot hear voices, but Flip Pallot, one of the great shallow-water fishermen, takes no chances. He talks in a whisper, especially when he is stalking a trophy bonefish or big tarpon. He notes that it is vital to be conscious of sound continuously and whispering helps him to do that.

When other boats are fishing a flat, you must be exceptionally careful about the direction from which you enter. Bonefish, for example, feed into the tide. If you approach from a position downtide of the second boat, you will probably spook the fish the other fishermen hope to find. Tarpon follow definite paths and if you interrupt their progress, you will destroy the fishing for those who are waiting or searching in the right place.

Leaving a flat is as important as entering it. The more fish are frightened, the warier they become. Flush them too many times and they may not come back. The angler who cranks the motor to leave and put-puts off the flat could be spoiling the fishing for others. It is not the best way to make friends. Even if you are alone and no one is watching, you should pole to deeper water before cranking the engine. Then, move slowly under power until you are in the channel and ready to go.

POLING

The lesson was brought home the hard way but never forgotten. Fishing for bonefish, we stayed shallow and followed the rising water over newly flooded territory. It seemed logical to us, but we saw only a few fish. That night, one of the local guides told us about the numerous bonefish he and his party saw on a neighboring flat. We pressed for details. Apparently the fish did not come up very high on the flat but stayed in deeper water that day. Had we poled properly, we probably would have found the fish.

Unless you know exactly where the fish will be, poling should follow a zigzag pattern that covers water of various depths. Move the boat in and out, constantly searching for your quarry. If you watch a guide, you'll see that he doesn't pole directly for a distant cloud without any variation. He may follow the edge of a flat and look across it or get high and gaze toward the edge.

If you can put wind and tide at your back and still have the sun in the proper place, you have it made. The primary consideration, of course, is the sun, because it affects visibility. If the sun is coming from one side or the other, position yourself so that it is behind you. Once in a while, scout the water behind you to see if you passed anything up or if fish are following you.

In the days when he was guiding, Stu Apte was as determined to chase fish as anyone we ever saw. He would lean on the pushpole and expend every ounce of energy to follow a school of fish. At first it looked futile to us, but more times than not he would intercept those fish and get a shot at them. It is

Angler has made a cast and the guide directs his retrieve from his higher elevation where he can see better.

not impossible to follow a school. That's another way of saying that you shouldn't give up just because fish seem far away or you have passed them. Of course if the school is spooked, forget them. We are talking about fish that have not been alerted or alarmed.

While you are poling, you must also search the water. It is easy for beginners to forget about their quarry and concentrate on where to put the

Poling a boat is not really hard work most of the time, if you do it right. Here a guide shows how to shift the pole properly from one side to the other.

Pole is brought behind guide without removing lower end from the water.

pushpole or how to steer the boat. Minds tend to wander and the heat of the day and the reflections of the clouds can deaden the senses. There is really no sense in covering territory if you don't do it effectively and efficiently.

Learning to pole is not difficult, but you should spend a little time practicing how to steer the boat and how to make it go straight. An unintended zigzag course across a flat is frustrating. If possible, a boat should be poled bow first and you must be able to handle the pole from either side of the stern if you do not have a platform. The pole usually is placed on the

Pole has been carried behind the guide to his other side and is ready to be used. Swinging a pole inside the boat can cause problems.

downwind or downcurrent side—whichever is stronger—and then turned to steer the boat. Anticipation is the key, just as it is when you guide a boat under power.

Poling should be done at a modest pace. If you work too hard just to scout the area, you will never have the energy to pursue fish or get into position. Expert polers put a caster in the precise spot to get a good shot at the fish. This is particularly important when fly fishing. Try to use the wind to the caster's advantage.

If the fish are coming toward you, it may be necessary to stop the boat by pushing the pole into the bottom or even poling backwards in order to maintain a distance between the boat and the fish. That extra time gives the fish a chance to eyeball the offering and strike it before the boat is seen.

THINGS TO KEEP IN MIND

Finding fish on your own takes a certain dedication and mental discipline. The more factors affecting the fishing that you can remember, the better your chances of succeeding. As an example, if you are traveling a long distance, a call ahead to check weather conditions may prove helpful. When you get on the flats, a thermometer may be your most valuable tool. Take readings often, especially if you find the water to be marginally hot or cold. One guide we know keeps a thermometer in his livewell so he can take readings at any time without waiting.

On the flats, each boat requires a lot of room to operate. It is not like offshore fishing where an entire fleet will gather in a single spot. If someone has already laid claim to the place you want to fish, you will have to find another area. Under no circumstances should one roar up to the other boat to inquire about their ratio of success or to ask for information. A marine radio might bring you the answers, but if you disturb someone else's sport and spot, he may not take kindly to offering assistance.

Knowing the habits of the fish is always helpful. If you recognize that tarpon will follow the edge of a flat, preferring to be in slightly deeper water with the tide pushing them against the lip of the shallows, you may wish to find stake-out sites. Look for places where the natural curvature of the flat forms a point or a pocket. An area where a channel or deeper cut leads right up to the flat might be good. The boat should be positioned so that it is in very shallow water—less than two feet or so—and the deeper edge is right in front. Hang back just enough so you can cover the area with casts; don't let the boat drift over the edge or too close to it.

There are areas of sand on the ocean side of the Florida Keys that make it easy to see tarpon. Anglers often stake out above these and wait for the fish to come to them. It takes patience, but the action can be excellent. When you stake out, you must recognize that the position of the boat may have to be changed as the tide continues to rise or fall. With rising water, the fish may start to cut to the inside of your position, blocking either your vision or your ability to reach them with a cast. On a falling tide, you may have to move outward. Watch the pattern of water across the flat for clues.

It is not possible to learn vast areas of flats in a short period of time. If you are new to the game and have only a limited amount of time, spend it wisely. Get the advice of local people and pick a few flats to fish. Ask them where you should be at various stages of the tide so that you can fill the day. Afterwards you might try a little exploring on your own.

Always carry a detailed chart of the area you are going to fish. If you are working one flat and it seems barren, try one nearby. It is only a guess, but unless you know where to go, you may spend a lot of time going from one place to another and not be any better off. One helpful suggestion is to note your success or failure on the charted flat, along with tide conditions. Eventually, the chart will become your bible.

Working tropical flats is a different ball game. You can master it if you take the time to do it systematically and concentrate on seeing fish. Without dedication, observation, and hard work, your successes will be minimal: still you should have a good time trying. There is no substitute for experience and gaining it produces some memorable events, with stories to match.

6 · Fly Fishing

THE FLATS WERE DESIGNED FOR FLY ROD FISHING. Since the water is shallow, reaching the fish in terms of depth shouldn't be a problem. All of the species you encounter will eat a fly well and some, like the tarpon, prefer it to any other artificial bait. Fly fishing is a deadly technique once you master the basics.

For the fresh water convert, a few adjustments are necessary. For one thing, you will be using heavier tackle than you did on stream or river and for another, you will have to cast farther. Remember that speed and accuracy are the keys to success. You have to get the fly to the fish immediately. The fish is on the move and will be out of range or will see you if the presentation is delayed.

THE CAST

There is no question that if you can cast 50 feet, you can catch fish on the flats. World records have been established on shorter casts than that. However, we believe that every angler should strive to perfect his casting techniques and increase the distance he can reach. The person who can put a fly 80 feet out has an advantage and anyone who can reach 100 feet, even with the wind at his back, gains that much more. Such an angler can make a more comfortable presentation at 50 or 60 feet than the one who has to grunt, groan, and pray to reach that distance. Remember that conditions seldom allow you to cast downwind on the flats.

Equally important, one should practice shooting line on the backcast. It is necessary to gather casting speed and vital when fish appear abeam of you on the side you hold the rod, for it is then that you must present the fly on the backcast. Turning takes too long and you might spook the fish. At the same time, learn to make short, quick flips. Fish have a habit of suddenly appearing right beside the boat.

Tournament casters have failed miserably on the flats because they were unfamiliar with the quick release methods that are necessary for success.

When you step up on the casting platform, strip out just enough line to reach the fish. How much you pull off the reel depends on visibility, wind, and your own casting ability. Be honest and you will encounter fewer problems with loose line tangling at the wrong time.

Make a cast so that the entire line is on the water. Then, strip it back carefully, laying it on the deck to eliminate tangling. If there are obstructions on the boat, throw over them a fine mesh net that is weighted on the corners with rubber-core sinkers. A minnow seine works very well. Masking tape may also be helpful. Unless you clear the line with the initial cast, the front part will be on the bottom of the coil and you can count on it to tangle the first time you cast to a fish.

Pushing the boat pole in the water and tying off is a favorite method of anchoring the boat on a flat. For fly fishermen, the pole should be set at a low angle to prevent the backcast from tangling in the pole.

When only 15 to 20 feet of line extend beyond the tip top of the rod, lift the tip and catch the fly in your hand. It should be held by the hackle behind the hook or at the bend of the hook. That will prevent the fly from inadvertently going into your hand when you start to make the cast and are only thinking about the fish. The rod is held in the casting hand with the fly line under the first or second finger and against the foregrip on the rod. The fly is held in the other hand.

Once you spot the fish, *don't take your eyes off it*. If you do, your vision may not pick it up again. Make a high forward roll cast, letting the fly be plucked from your fingers by the moving line. At the instant the fly is released, reach over and grasp the fly line in that hand. You can now double-haul and shoot line on the backcast. With practice, the second forward cast should enable you to get the fly to the fish. If you do not have line speed or control of the loop, one more backcast and forward cast may be required. That is all it should take, however, even if you want to cast 100 feet.

No one can do this without practice and the place to train is on a lawn, in a park, or somewhere other than the flats when a fish is in front of you. All good flats fishermen have taken the time to perfect the system. Practice until you can deliver a good cast in no more than six seconds.

Fish on the flats have a habit of changing direction just about the time you release the line and try to shoot the fly. Beginners tend to pause, hoping the fish will reverse course and ultimately see the fly. That is a mistake. A better approach is to simply pick up all the fly line without stripping in and drop it in front of the fish again. If you stop to strip in, you are wasting precious time.

In order to pick up a lot of line, you must reach as far forward as you can and haul just as the fly is about to clear the surface of the water. There should be no false casting. You have plenty of line in the air and can go right back to the fish.

Speed and accuracy have been the bywords for flats fishing over the years, but there are limitations. We believe it is far better for an angler to work at a comfortable speed than to rush a cast. Increased speed of delivery comes with practice. If you are slow, you will miss opportunities, but that is better than trying to get a fly air-borne in panic—or cutting it out of the back of your neck.

THE RETRIEVE

Assuming you placed the fly in front of and beyond the fish and you allowed it to sink to the proper depth, the next task is the retrieve. Those who were trained in a fresh water environment may feel compelled to weave the line around their fingers or use the rod tip to manipulate the fly. Both of these practices lead to trouble. In the first instance and if the fish takes the fly, you will never clear the line from your fingers. By using the rod tip, you lose the advantage of being in position to set the hook or make another cast.

The accepted method is to put the butt of the rod at your belt buckle with the tip pointing directly at the fly line in the water and as close to the surface as possible. Hold the rod in one hand with the line between your first or second finger and the grip. Reach behind the rod hand with your other hand and pick up the line. By pulling on the line with the second hand, you can

When stripping line, the rod should be pointed at the fly to eliminate all slack, obtain a better hook-up, and allow you more margin for striking with the rod.

make the fly do anything you want. A long, steady pull will swim it forward. Short tugs will cause it to make tiny forward spurts. The second hand controls the distance the fly travels and its speed.

If you must cast again, the line is already in the second hand and the rod tip is pointing at the spot in the water where the line enters. All you have to do is start the pickup and backcast and you can get the fly back to the fish.

A BREAK WITH TRADITION

We are about to look tradition right in the eye and throw down the gauntlet in three very important areas. The practices in question have been the accepted methods for a long time and there was a period when we were in total agreement with them. In reflecting on salt water fly fishing, however, we find our views changing on many things.

The salt water taper fly line has been extremely popular over the years because it was designed to allow anglers to obtain a quick presentation. To achieve this goal, manufacturers used a short front taper and concentrated the weight of the line in the first 25 feet instead of the first 30 feet. The theory was that with more weight placed forward, the line would be easier to cast, since you only had 15 to 20 feet of line extending past the tip top when you started.

Although the concept seemed sound, in practice the salt water taper (which probably should have been called a speed-casting taper) fell short of its goal. Compared to the sink-tip fly lines we have today, it is the more difficult with which to make a presentation.

In any sort of casting, as soon as the loop starts to open or unrolls completely, the fly line begins to fall. It happens to all lines regardless of density or taper. When the loop on a salt water taper opens, inertia causes the heavy, concentrated weight right behind the short front taper to continue forward. It actually overruns the lighter part and folds back under it, ruining the presentation. The front taper, leader, and fly are dumped into the water together and the cast collapses.

In re-evaluating the cast, we have come to believe that salt water tapers do not have much use in salt water. Unless you are a highly skilled caster, controlling these lines is difficult. Almost everyone is better off with a standard weight-forward line. You may require an extra false cast to get it to the fish, but you will have a better presentation and that is of critical importance.

Tarpon fishermen employ an intermediate or floating weight-forward fly line attached to several hundred yards of braided dacron backing. One of the biggest problems of tarpon fishing results from the jumps a hooked tarpon makes and the consequent need to push the rodtip forward and bow to the fish. If you don't, the weight and speed of the fish in the air will snap the leader like bakery string. The difficulty, of course, is in reacting quickly to the jump and throwing the controlled slack soon enough. Even with experience, that's not always easy to do.

Those who accept the challenge of sailfishing on a fly face the same problem. These fish sprint out beyond the fly line and then greyhound or skyrocket or otherwise dazzle you with aerial acrobatics. It takes intense concentration and good reflexes to be quick, to remember to bow.

Captain Jim Paddock and Captain Rick DeFeo showed us a solution to this problem on a fishing trip to Costa Rica back in the 1970's. They made special shooting heads that were about 60 feet long and attached 100 yards of 25-pound-test monofilament to the head. The other end of the mono was looped to the standard braided dacron backing. Because of its stretch factor, the monofilament acted as a giant shock absorber and helped to cushion the effects of those impressive jumps.

The same system can be used effectively on the flats for giant tarpon and for bruising sharks that charge across the shallows like an avalanche down a mountain. We recommend a shooting head made from an intermediate line or even a floating fly line. However, one could use the whole line and still resort to the monofilament shock absorber. High-visibility mono has an added advantage, which is that you can see it easily and maneuver the boat more accurately when you are chasing the fish. Try this system for tarpon and we guarantee you'll improve your score.

Who among us has not used a nail knot or needle knot to attach the butt section of the leader to the fly line? That has been the traditional method for countless years. Actually, butt sections are a carry over from dry fly fishing and gravitated to the salt quite naturally. Several seasons back while trout and salmon fishing, we experimented extensively with butt sections that measured three or four inches in length and found that we caught just as many fish as with longer butt sections. Eventually, we eliminated the nail knot when angling for trout and looped the leader tippet directly to the fly line.

That is precisely the system we advocate for most salt water fishing. The only purpose of a butt section and a long leader is to move the fly line away from the fish; it is much easier to cast four feet of leader than seven to nine feet. And if you have to pick a sinking line off the water, a short leader moves nicely. In the wind, the absence of a butt section helps the fly to turn over and you can certainly tuck cast a short leader under the mangroves with much more ease than a long one.

Fish see all leaders. If they ignore a 100-pound-test shock tippet, it won't make any difference if the leader has a butt section or not. There are a couple of exceptions. When tarpon are over white sand or are laid up early in the morning, it may be necessary to use a longer leader to move the impact of the fly line away from them. In bonefishing, a delicate presentation is usually mandatory, so a greater leader length should be used. Otherwise you are better off looping the tippet directly to the fly line.

The connection between tippet and the fly line is easy to make. Simply remove about a half inch of the coating from the end of the fly line. This is done by slipping 20-pound-test dacron or mono in a girth hitch around the line, cinching the hitch, and pulling the dacron, together with the coating, off the end of the fly line. You can also remove the coating by dipping the end of the fly line in acetone.

Take a needle and fray the end of the fly line core so that it opens. Lay this back against the rest of the line, thereby forming a small loop in the end of the fly line. Then, using a fly-tying bobbin and thread, serve the fly line and the core together to secure the loop. A coating of rubber cement will prevent it from snagging or the thread from coming loose. Before you fish, test all the loops for strength by pulling on them. They must, of course, be wrapped under moderate pressure if they are to hold.

With a Bimini Twist in the end of the leader tippet and a double surgeon's loop to double the Bimini, you can interlock the two loops. To change leaders is easy. Simply unlock the loops and you are ready to put the next one on.

Fishing conditions will dictate the length of the leader. As long as the impact of the line on the water does not frighten the fish, it is to your advantage to use a shorter leader. You'll also be pleased to know that correctly tied loops that are properly interlocked seldom seem to fail or tangle.

While we are on the subject of leaders, there are a few other facts worth noting. If you should catch a world-record fish and want it to be accepted by the International Game Fish Association, the leader tippet must be at least 15 inches long. As the breaking strength of the tippet decreases, its length should increase. That means that by the time you are down to an eight-pound-test tippet, you may choose a length of twenty-four or even thirty inches. The reason for this is that the longer length has additional stretch and is therefore more forgiving.

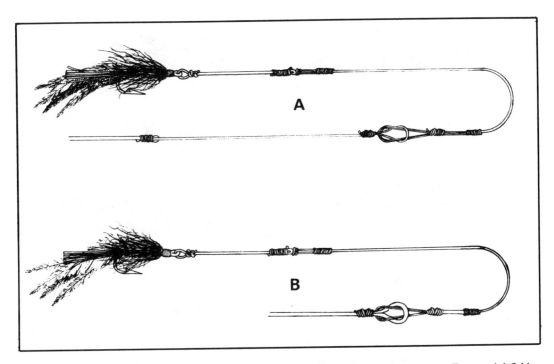

Two basic leaders for salt-water fly fishing, where a shock leader of heavy monofilament or wire is required. Let's look at Figure A. Beginning at the first knot at the hook eye: often a free-swinging knot, such as Homer Rhodes' Loop Knot or a similar one, is used in the heavy shock leader of braided wire or monofilament. Then comes the shock leader. This is connected to a Bimini Twist knot with one of several connections—the Albright is the most popular. Then comes the class tippet (the weakest section of the leader), with a Bimini Twist tied in the other end of the tippet. This Bimini is then tied into a Surgeon's Loop and joined to a section of 30- to 40-pound monofila-ment, usually 3 to 4 feet long. For special fishing situations (such as tarpon over white sand), the butt section may be 10 to 12 feet in length.

Figure B is identical in construction to Figure A with one exception. The butt section has been eliminated and the Surgeon's Loop in the Bimini portion of the tippet is looped directly to the fly line. This allows the lure to turn over better and makes it easier to lift the fly from the water, especially when using a slow-sink or fast-sinking line. We have used this method for a number of years and in almost all situations where a heavy shock leader is used, it is advantageous to eliminate the butt section.

SOME THOUGHTS ON FLIES

Whether they are in eighteen inches or ten feet of water, fish feed best when the fly is at eye level or close enough to reach easily. Fish seldom descend to take a fly, but they will rise for it. The sink rate of the fly is one of the most critical factors in flats fishing, yet it is frequently overlooked. Regardless of where the fish is searching for food, you want the fly to be on a collision course with it.

If you are fishing redfish in very shallow water, a Palmer-tied fly with heavy hackle that keeps it close to the surface will stay in front of the fish and

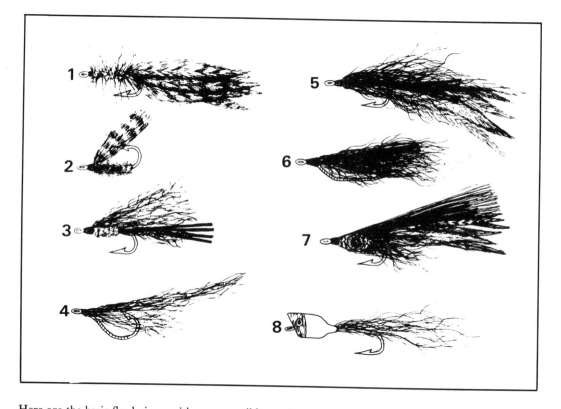

Here are the basic fly designs, with some possible variations in each category: (1) Basic hackle streamer, one of the oldest known fly patterns. (2) Reverse-tied wing fly—more than 80 percent of all bonefish flies are tied in this manner; they're valuable in cases where you want the hook to ride up to prevent snagging in weeds and bottom. (3) Joe Brooks' Blonde series. (4) Bent-back, popularized by Chico Fernandez and an answer to the Keel-hook-type fly that many prefer. (5) Lefty's Deceiver, a style of fly that casts well, swims nicely, and resembles baitfish in shape—there are many color variations of this pattern. (6) Keel hook fly; this specially designed hook allows you to fish many areas where other standard patterns would snag on bushes, limbs, grass, or bottom. (7) Basic streamer, but with a large eye painted on a feather. Streamers with larger eyes are becoming more popular. (8) A standard popping bug. Note clearance between hook point and body. The slider is the same bug, but with the tapered portion of the bug facing forward. This allows you to work an almost silent bug on the surface in the shallows, which is often better than a standard popper, which creates a lot of noise that would frighten the fish.

Mono loop weed guard on a popper which can also be used on streamer flies, was popularized by Ted Trueblood of *Field and Stream* in the early 1950s, but has only recently caught on. The monofilament for most salt-water flies should be 20-or 30-pound soft material. The loop stays in position better if the wraps are carried down to the point indicated by the arrows, and then coated with either paint or epoxy glue. Mono loop weed guards allow you to fish many areas where Keel hooks would be required, and some fishermen feel they get more hook-ups on the strike with them.

perhaps tease it into striking. A fly that sinks may be lost in the grass and never seen by your quarry. The same fly would fail miserably with a tarpon in seven feet of water, because it would never get down to the fish in time.

Sink rate is determined by several factors that include the size and type of hook (heavy wire or light wire), the type and length of the dressing, amount of material, leader length, and even the type of fly line. Sometimes you want the fly to sink very slowly and at others you need a fly that will plummet quickly. The important point is that you know the sink rate of the fly you are using.

Unless you have that knowledge, you do not really know how far in front of the fish to cast. Although fish on the flats don't seem to be moving very quickly, they have a habit of closing the gap in short order. If you are going to err in depth, it's better to have the fly slightly above then below the fish. With the exception of bonefish, most species will rise for a fly rather than dip down for one. Bonefish are used to feeding on the bottom and therefore are concentrating on the zone below them.

Successful fishermen learn as much as they can about the species they seek. You should know that tarpon prefer a slow retrieve, while bonefish merely need to see some semblance of life in the fly. It can almost be "ticked" in place and a bonefish will pounce on it. Jacks and barracuda respond best to a fast-moving fly. When it comes to permit, you're on your own.

Whenever there is a choice, the presentation should be made upcurrent for fish that feed into the tide. That way, the fly will sweep toward them in a natural manner. It is almost like the greased-line technique in salmon fishing. Anytime the fly is presented in full silhouette, you have a better chance of scoring.

Night fishing suggests different priorities. A fly with a bulky head that pushes water and can be heard under the surface will produce more strikes. The same theory holds for stripers in San Francisco Bay as it does for tarpon in the channels or ladyfish around the bridges.

We have been convinced for a long time that eyes on a fly enhance its appeal. It doesn't matter whether you paint them on or use felt-tip markers or any other device. The eye has always been an important target for predators. Nature's camouflage for certain fish species includes false spots that look like eyes, apparently to make the predator think that the tail is the head and vice versa. If the flies you use do not have pronounced eyes, we urge you to do the job yourself. You might even want to run a few comparisons. Some model airplane dope and the flat head of a nail will produce an eye. A second color of paint and a smaller nail puts a pupil in the eye.

MAKING IT EASIER

A boat not only gets you to the fish, but it becomes your casting platform once you are on the scene. Using it to your advantage when fly casting takes a little bit of thought. As a basic rule, only one person should fly cast at a time in a small boat. Experts sometimes violate this, but it makes sense to take turns and not risk hooking someone with an errant fly.

Wind is always a serious consideration. If possible, the boat should be maneuvered so that the fly line stays clear of all hands on both the forward cast and the backcast. In addition, the cast should be outboard and over the water as much as possible. This often can be achieved by angling the boat or by placing the fly caster in either bow or stern depending on wind direction.

When blind casting from a drifting boat, there is a tendency to cast with the wind. Obviously, this produces longer casts, but it also has a negative effect. Since the boat is drifting in that direction, there is little time for a retrieve. One has to hurry to recover line.

A better solution is to cast across the wind. Let's assume you are standing in the bow of a skiff and the west wind is striking the port side. You would be casting in the direction the bow is pointing which, in this example, is north. The wind blows at right angles and tends to keep the fly line outboard and over your right shoulder. If you are a left-handed caster, you would want to cast from the stern and direct your cast to the south.

When you are being poled in a boat, the loop of fly line between the fly in your hand and the rod tip must not reach back where the pushpole is entering the water. Otherwise, the pole may slip into the long loop and pull the fly from your hand. If you insist on more fly line past the tip top, be sure it loops on the side opposite the poling side. Also be careful that floating grass doesn't hang in the loop trailing in the water. On boats with poling platforms over the engine, the problem is usually eliminated.

A fly rod has no rear handle, and many people install a short butt section. We feel that any butt extension longer than three inches is usually more trouble than it's worth. One of the most comfortable and useful butt sections is the rubber one at top that is slipped over the seat after the reel is in place. The lower butt section is cork, and works well, but would be more comfortable if it were more round.

Some reels that will work well on the flats for all but very large fish, such as tarpon and sharks. Top row, left to right: Gehrke's Marryat and Garcia's Diplomat, Model 178; center is Pflueger Medalist (an old standby); and bottom row, left to right: Valentine and the now discontinued Scientific Anglers reel. Hardy, who made this reel offers a similar model in five sizes called Sunbeam.

The Pflueger Medalist is perhaps the best known single-action reel in the world. It is relatively inexpensive and with care can be used for years in salt water.

If you are spot casting to a fish, it is well to try keeping the fly clear of the boat, but primary responsibility for getting out of the way rests with the guide and anyone else aboard. That may mean that the other angler has to get down on the deck or find whatever cover is available. Although the fly caster should be aware of others, they must remain alert to a fly going through the air like a buzzsaw.

Three of the most popular reels for fighting any fish you'll encounter on the flats: at top is the Seamaster, which comes in a number of sizes and with slip clutch and direct drive. Bottom left, is Fin/Nor, with the same features as Seamaster. Bottom right is a Billy Pate Reel, with slip clutch only. All three reels are handmade, expensive, and worth every penny you pay for them.

POINTS TO REMEMBER

A decade ago, writers were insisting that bonefishermen had to use a fly-fishing outfit capable of handling a 9-weight line and that flies should be tied on a 1/0 hook. Modern-day specialists have opted for lighter rods and lines because of the importance of a delicate presentation. They may not be able to cast as far with a rod matched to a 4-weight, 5-weight, 6-weight, or 7-weight line, but they catch more fish in many situations because the line landing on the water does not frighten their quarry. Nowadays flies are tied on numbers 2, 4, or 6 hooks and sometimes number 8.

There are two important adaptations that will make the reel more useful on the flats. A large hole has been made in the sideplate. When a fish is hooked the thumb or fingertips can be inserted in the hole and forced against the spool side to obtain the desired drag. This works exceptionally well and we have taken several tarpon exceeding 50 pounds on this reel. The other feature is a stainless steel ¼ x 20 nut, glued on with epoxy, which balances the handle of the reel. This removes vibration from an out-of-balance reel when a fish makes a fast run.

Nothing dramatizes the nervousness of fish on the flats more than the responses of husky sharks ranging from six to eight feet in length. If the fly line splats on the water too close to the fish, it will panic and flush. Their jaws carry the dental armament necessary for protection, yet they flee from the

Dan Blanton shows three fly-fishing outfits, completely rigged with flies attached to leaders. The outfits have been stored in homemade rip-stock nylon sacks. The ones in use can be kept out of the way but ready when needed—if you don't have good rod holders in the boat.

Most experienced flats fishermen use a minimum of mechanical drag on the reel, and obtain additional drag by using the hands and fingers. The advantage to this is that by removing the fingers they can instantly remove drag pressure as fish surges away from them.

Here the angler is using his fingertips on the inside of the reel spool to get the extra pressure he needs.

You can also use the finger of the hand holding the rod to trap the line against the rod, resulting in additional drag, but the finger can be removed at will. With slip-clutch type drags, when lifting a fish near the boat, this finger can help prevent slippage as the heavy fish is lifted.

slightest sound. If a shark behaves in this way, think of the reaction from bonefish, tarpon, permit, bluefish, and other denizens of the flats.

The calmer the water and the more gentle the wind, the longer the leader you will need. When the flats are slick, bonefish are more difficult to approach and tarpon over white sand may be as skittish as a long-tailed cat in a room full of rocking chairs. That is when you must think of lengthening the leaders, reducing the size of the fly line, and casting well in front of the fish.

Although the following technique was developed with shooting heads, particularly those that sink, it works with any fly line. If you are blind casting

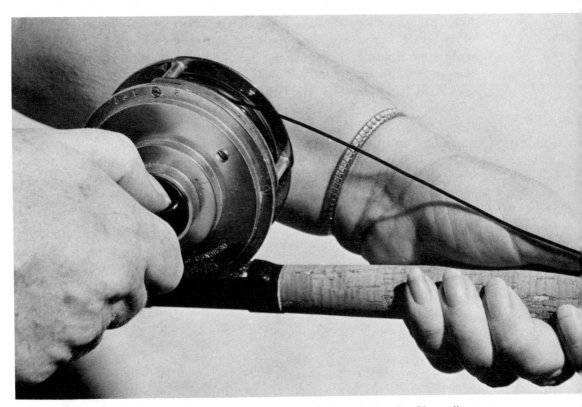

Some reels have the drag-adjustment nut on the opposite side from the handle. If an adjustment is made during the fight, this placement can be difficult. However, by simply turning the reel upside down, you can easily make the adjustment. Be sure you turn the drag in the right direction—practice at home.

and want to cover as much water as possible, you can use the water-haul method. All you have to do is throw a weak forward cast, letting the line fall on the surface of the water. Then make the regular pickup, shoot a little line on the backcast, and let it go on the forward cast. The surface tension of the water on the line being lifted will load the rod and you'll be amazed by the extra distance in your second cast. Of course, if fish are close by, the line landing on the water the first time may frighten them.

Being observant on the water and concentrating on what works best for you will make you a better fly fisherman. No one can practice for you nor can anyone help when you are standing on the casting platform in a one-on-one confrontation with the fish. Here is the supreme test. Even though your knees may be vibrating like a tuning fork and excitement has opened the valve on your adrenalin, the key is to remain cool and try to function effectively. It is easier said than done but must be the goal of every fly fisherman. Pushing the cast will usually spoil the presentation, so remember to cast at a comfortable speed even though you are late in getting the fly to the fish.

Understand too that not every set of conditions on the water is conducive to fly fishing. There are days when, for a variety of reasons, it pays to use other tackle. It is a wise angler who recognizes these times and switches to more appropriate gear. Trying to force the fly rod usually results in frustration and disappointment. There will be other days.

With fly patterns that are designed to be practically weedless you may be able to fish a fly where other lures will hang in the grass. If you have selected the sink rate carefully, you can keep a fly in front of a fish longer than any other lure and move it at a teasingly slow pace. When fish are in shallow water, a fly can be made to parachute down and land as gently as a feather. That means you can present it nearer the fish without alarming your quarry. Besides, fly patterns frequently imitate bait fish more closely than anything else other than the natural.

If you plan to hire a guide—always a wise decision—shop around until you find one who specializes in fly fishing. He can share his expertise with you and help you to master many of these techniques quickly. Still, in spite of good intentions and careful precautions, things sometimes go wrong and problems are compounded. If it's any consolation, all of us have been through it.

7 · Spinning and Plug

Picture yourself standing atop a casting platform as you are being poled silently across a flat aboard a skiff that almost can float in heavy dew. A panorama of unique scenery unfolds before your eyes as you look through the surface of the water and study every bottom configuration. Suddenly, you focus on a moving shadow ghosting along just above the turtle grass. It is going from right to left and you only have seconds to get a lure in front of it.

This is a typical flats situation, yet countless anglers armed with desire and enthusiasm fail the test daily. They may have used spinning or plug-casting gear for years, but they have always had the luxury of time on their side and they were never required to lead a moving target.

If guides were willing to level with you, they would confess that their most emphatic gripe is the inability of customers to get a bait or lure in front of a fish within the allotted time. It is frustrating to put someone in casting position over and over again and have him flub the cast.

The answer, of course, lies in practice, but it is equally important to know what to practice and how. Keep in mind that one should not wait until he is at the fishing site to think about learning. That must be done well in advance. Surprisingly, those who already have the most experience on the flats are constantly working to improve their techniques. And if it is any incentive, guides tend to work harder (unconsciously or even consciously) when they know they have an angler who can perform under pressure.

CASTING TECHNIQUES

Before you concern yourself with the proper way to cast, you should hone your ability to open the bail and pick up the line on a spinning reel or depress the freespool button on a plug reel without looking. Every second counts.

Remember that your eyes will be on the fish. Never look away, even for an instant, once you have the target in sight.

The way to practice is to make a cast. Then, reel in as quickly as you can turn the handle, because that is exactly what you have to do if your first presentation is off-target. If you spin your wrist as you turn the handle on the reel, the revolutions are faster than if you allow your whole arm to rotate. The instant the lure is near the tip top, open the bail or push the freespool lever and make another cast. In the process, you will also learn to allow the right amount of overhang past the tip top.

No matter how light the rod, all casting should be done with two hands on the grip. You may have to push your fists together as if the grip were a baseball bat, but you can get both hands on even an ultra-light if you try.

In order to cast accurately, you must control the line of flight to the target and then adjust the distance. The easiest way to accomplish this is to face the target squarely. Your eyes should be focused on the spot you want to hit. Bring the rod up sharply in a direct line right between your eyes. Then, come forward and release. You may have to cast a heavy plug outfit from one side, but the line of the cast should be parallel to that of your vision. A one-handed plug outfit for smaller fish should be cast by first bringing it up to your face.

The basic cast eliminates any sidearm swings or angles that cut across the vertical. With spinning in particular, it is simple to snap-cast in a direct line. This form of casting also creates a flat trajectory if you release precisely. Casts that skyrocket from an early release will be blown off-course if there is any wind. Those that crash-dive indicate that you released too late.

The whole procedure is very similar to instinctive shooting. Your eye holds the target and your hands respond. Adjusting for distance is nothing more than feathering the spool of a spinning outfit to slow and stop the line or thumbing the spool of plug gear.

Three popular spinning reels for bonefish, sea trout, baby tarpon, snook, bluefish, and similar fish. Top is Shimano's MLX, which allows the angler to open the bail with one of the fingers on the hand holding the rod, speeding up a second cast. Lower left is the Abu 754 and right is Daiwa's PS 13. Both models are extremely light. Portions of the reels are constructed from graphite and all are top quality.

Reel on left has a standard bail. Reel on right is the same model, but has been modified to take a Garcia manual ball-bearing roller. It takes perhaps a half an hour to get used to fishing with a manual bail, but it has many advantages. It is faster to make the second cast, bail springs are unnecessary, it works everytime, and the roller always rolls—important considerations when fighting tough fish on light lines.

Not every fish bursts into view at a distance. Shallow water work demands that you react quickly to sudden targets, much as you would on a shooting range when a target pops up. For that reason, it pays to practice your accuracy with side flips, over-the-shoulder casts, and short casts.

When you are fishing, your outfit should always be in the ready position. That means that the bail is open on spinning tackle and you are holding the line on your forefinger primed to respond in an instant. With plug tackle, the reel is in freespool and your thumb is against the spool. The right amount of overhang extends beyond the tip top.

Arrows indicate the center of the reel spool. It is necessary only to push the line past the center of the spool to hold it in readiness for casting. Gripping the line tightly against the rod handle often results in a poor release and a bad cast.

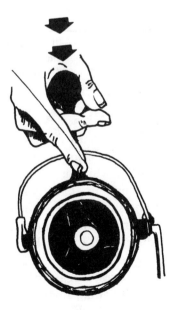

When you first reach the fishing spot, make a practice cast or two to get the feel of the tackle and to lay the line on the reel smoothly. As you retrieve and practice cast, let the line run between your thumb and forefinger as you apply a slight amount of pressure. The line then has been spooled under a little tension and will come off nicely when you make a presentation. Besides, a wet line is less prone to tangle or backlash.

If you happen to be using live bait, it must be healthy and frisky when you make the cast. Novices sometimes become so intent on scouting the flats that they let the bait at the end of their lines dangle out of the water. It should be kept in the water right alongside the boat until you are ready to cast. Drop the rod tip as you do this so that the correct amount of overhang extends beyond the tip. That way, you only have to pick up and cast since the bail is already open or the reel is in freespool.

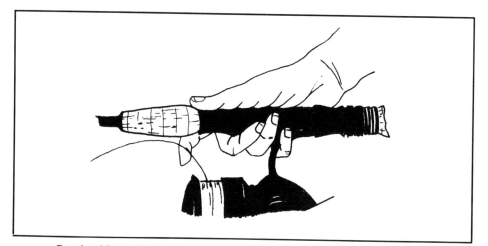

People with small hands (including children and women) should place three or even all four fingers in front of the reel post in order to be able to catch the line easily with the first finger.

RIGGING

Most marine fish boast teeth, sharp gill covers, abrasive backs, or habitually rub their snouts against something that will fray line. They are not leader-shy, which is reason enough to use a heavier shock leader. We are going to assume that if you are casting, you are using 20-pound-test line or less. The shock leader should be directly tailored for the species you seek.

Seatrout, for example, have soft mouths, won't burrow in the bottom, and their teeth cannot be compared to those of the bluefish. A light shock tippet would make sense, but you don't need anything to withstand extreme circumstances. It really doesn't hurt if you use a shock leader of 20-pound-test or even 30-pound. Bonefish guides do this, although we prefer a much lighter shock for bonefish if we use any at all.

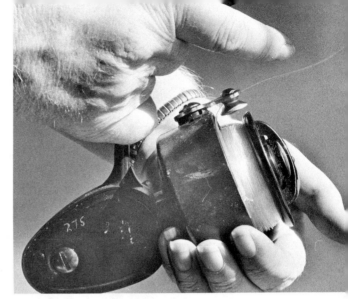

When fighting a big fish, it may become necessary to apply more drag. Pressing the fingertip against the spool side, or palming the reel spool, as shown, allows you to place additional restraint on the escaping fish. But, if necessary, the hand can be removed immediately so that the fish is straining only against the lighter mechanically adjusted drag.

For almost all spin casting in salt water the use of the second hand on the lower part of the rod will allow you to develop more tip speed, throw heavier lures, and increase your distance. The two-handed cast is a must on the flats in many situations.

During a long fight it may become necessary to rest your arm, but you want to continue applying pressure on the fish. Placing the rod handle against your arm as shown here can be helpful.

The line can be attached to the shock leader via a small black swivel or you can tie it directly. If you do not know the Bimini Twist, you should learn it, since it is the heart of any light-tackle leader system. The Spider Hitch is a poor alternative, but must be considered better than nothing. Either of these knots will double the end of the lighter line. Then, all you need is a double surgeon's knot to connect to the heavier shock leader.

"Feeling" a jig that's being retrieved is a skill many never develop, but knowing when a fish has lightly grabbed a jig can increase your score of hook-ups. One way with plug reels is to let the line flow across the sensitive area on the thumb, as shown here. Every tap is then felt.

When a tarpon or shark first takes and then swims directly away from you, your line is probably stretched across its back. Small-diameter monofilament will not last very long in this situation, especially when the fish is six feet long. Here is where a two-stage leader comes into play. Tie a six- to eight-foot length of forty- or fifty-pound test mono to your fishing line. Then attach a relatively short, heavy shock leader to that. The combination will protect against fraying at the mouth and also give you a cushion against the roughness of the fish's back.

The huskier leader also gives you something to grab when the fish gets near the boat and you have to handle it. One word of caution. Unless the tip top on the rod is large, knots and swivels will not pass through it. That is why the shock leader has to be short. If it is too long, you won't be able to cast comfortably.

Barracuda and sharks can bite through any monofilament. Wire is the only answer. However, do not use an excessive length of wire, which makes it more difficult to cast bait or lure, deprives the offering of a natural action, and turns the fish away. With barracuda, you only need three or four inches of small-diameter wire such as #3. Sharks may require a slightly longer piece, especially if you are feeding them bait. Still, it should be the shortest length possible under the circumstances.

If you are fishing bluefish, opt for 50- to 80-pound monofilament instead of wire in clear waters. It is a better choice and will elicit more strikes. Occasionally, a hefty blue may chop through it, but it is worth the risk.

OPPORTUNITY FISHING

Although some fishermen prefer to specialize in one species or another, you can add an extra dimension to flats action by keeping a number of rods rigged for whatever comes along. Even if you decide to ignore everything except the species you have in mind, you should have one or two additional rods ready to go.

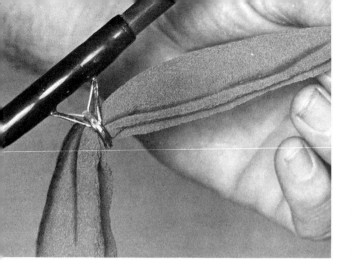

Ceramic or aluminum oxide guides are super smooth and wear very well. However, they can get a hairline crack in them that cuts line like a razor blade. A quick check for cracks can be made by drawing a section of discarded pantyhose through the guide. Any broken or cracked area will grab and snag the pantyhose.

These extra rods must be kept where you can get to them easily. If you are fishing bait, you might want to have an artifical ready to cast. Even if you are presently using a lure, tie a different one on the back-up outfit. That gives you the advantage of trying something else without taking the time to rig again. You also are ready in the event of a break-off.

Assuming you are bonefishing, you might have a rod with a tube lure for barracuda, another with a darting plug for sharks, and a third with an offering for tarpon or permit. There is no time to make changes or adjustments when you suddenly spot the fish. The best you can hope for is a moment to grab the back-up rod and make the cast. Drags should already be set so that you merely pick up the rod and cast.

There are going to be times when a species appears and you are not rigged for it. When that happens, your only chance is to gamble on what you have. Even without a leader, you can have fun hooking the fish and it certainly gives you the opportunity to practice your casting.

On the other hand, there is a special flats discipline worth discussing. You are tarpon fishing and spot a barracuda. Instinctively, you want to cast to it, but the guide tells you not to do it. The reason may not be clear, but experience shows that about the time that 'cuda is tearing up the flats and you are trying to land it, a school of the biggest and meanest tarpon that ever prowled the shallow flats suddenly shows and you are caught between the proverbial rock and hard place. If you want to fish for anything that comes along, make that perfectly clear to the guide and your fishing partner beforehand. Your friend may have his heart set on the primary species and not want anything to come between him and his goal.

Using the same philosophy, you can get more out of fishing the flats if you learn to handle all forms of tackle. It's fun to switch off between spinning and plug and, when conditions are right, to toss a fly to a cruising fish.

THE TARGET

There are no mysteries in flats fishing. You see the fish and you know where the lure is at every moment. Response becomes a factor that can be measured visually, leaving no doubt in your mind. If a lure lands too close, the fish is gone instantly. If the path of the bait or artificial does not cross the

This is the leader box closed and ready for use. A section of rubber from an innertube, glued to the inside and with the leader pulled through a hole, prevents the line from slipping back into the box. Also, by placing some Velcro on the base of the box, and gluing some on the boat console in the proper place, you can install the box where it's handy, and remove it easily when you want.

vision of the fish, it will not be seen. Each situation demands a quick decision, but the parameters are constantly changing.

Fish may be coming directly toward you, closing in at a rapid rate. They may be lingering in one area without much progress in any direction. Sometimes your quarry will move straight away from you. On other occasions, it may cross from left to right or right to left. Or it may take off at an oblique angle.

Veterans refer to it as "lining a fish" and it is nothing more than casting so that the lure falls ahead of the target, but the line drops across one or more fish. That may be all it takes to chase an entire school to another flat. The

Attaché boxes are perfect for the traveling angler. Carry several of them with lures for particular places or species in individual boxes. Also, get one deep enough to carry spare spinning reel spools. A nice feature is that most of these boxes will fit in a large, soft duffle-type traveling bag, which most experienced anglers prefer.

ultimate goal is for the fish to see the bait or lure without realizing that anything is amiss. Sometimes, the sight of a light- or bright-colored fly line unrolling in the air will line a fish. Colors such as gray, medium-blue, or green help to prevent this.

When a school of fish is swimming directly away from you and you don't think you can intercept them with the boat, you have to gamble. Try to place the cast to one side of the school and to get the offering ahead of them. If all else fails, you may have to line them, but that should be the last resort.

Fish moving directly toward you can be very deceptive. It often looks as if they are barely underway, but usually the closing rate is much faster than you think. Many casters put the lure too close to the fish, simply because they lead as if the fish were stationary. By the time the lure lands, the school has closed the gap and is under it.

With your quarry moving down on you, it is better to err on the side of more lead rather than less lead. You can always let the bait or lure drop to the bottom and wait. When the fish are almost to it, start it moving as if the predator flushed the prey. You may have to increase the retrieve rate if boat and fish are closing.

Situations in which the fish are moving at right angles to you seem to be the easiest. If you cast in front of the fish, you can drag the offering along in front of the whole school. Equally important, they have a broadside view of the bait and can rush forward to grab it without changing direction.

When a fish swims away obliquely at a 45° angle, the cast should be on the inside between you and the fish. In other words, if you are standing in the bow and the fish is heading to the right oblique, you should cast to the right side of the fish. The line won't cross his back and it's an easier cast. If the fish is easing off to the left, put the lure on the left side.

No self-respecting game fish expects its prey to attack it. When that happens, the husky predator usually retreats and re-groups. He knows something is not natural. This is precisely why your bait or lure must move across the path of the fish or angle away from it. Anything that can be eaten wants to get out of the way. When you think about it, casting directly in front of a school going away from you or swimming at an oblique angle makes it tougher to get a strike. The only retrieve you have is directly toward the fish. Certainly they clobber bait from instinct, but it does not happen as often as it does at another angle. In those situations, try to keep the lure to one side or the other and a fish may peel off and grab it.

It is worth noting, again, that tackle for flats fishing should be kept in prime condition. Lines must be changed frequently and the condition of the reel checked daily. This is a demanding sport where all the pieces of the puzzle must fall into place. Nowhere will you find a greater challenge. It's up to you to be ready for it.

8 · Tarpon: The Silver King

If you ask a group of leading flats anglers to name their favorite flats fish, most will point to the tarpon without hesitation. Suggest that they then name the second most exciting fish and, to a man, they will have to pause and think.

Tarpon come in two sizes: small and large. Giant tarpon give a person everything he needs in a fish. It's visual fishing packed with excitement. The quarry is hunted and caught on relatively light tackle, yet will weigh in excess of a hundred pounds and span six feet or more in length. The girth can be staggering. Most importantly, the whole game is played out where you can watch every step from the presentation through the strike and the ensuing battle.

Although the silver king is caught from Virginia to Texas, the most serious flats fishing takes place from lower Biscayne Bay in Miami down along the Florida Keys to Key West and the Dry Tortugas. Plenty of action occurs in Florida Bay, up through the 10,000 Islands, and along the West Coast of Florida to the area around Homasassa. Outside the United States, tarpon fishing can be enjoyed along the Gulf side of Mexico and in several spots through the Caribbean and Central America. The ultimate sport takes place on those clear-water flats where one stalks the fish. The extra dimension of visibility has no parallel in blind casting. Tarpon may battle just as hard in turbid water, but it is not the same game.

KNOWING THE QUARRY

Even on the flats, tarpon fishing has several dimensions. Usually, they will be in three to ten feet of water prowling alone, in pods of two or three, or in schools of several fish. Channels become the highways and resting points.

Nothing is prettier or more graceful than the gill-rattling leaps of an irate tarpon.

Tarpon may work the downtide end of a channel before getting up on a flat or after coming off a flat.

Very early in the morning, they may lie motionless in the shallows with dorsal and tail puncturing the surface or they may nestle on the bottom in the various basins. These are difficult fish to approach, but they will eat readily if fly, lure, or bait is on-target.

Most tarpon fishing is done from a skiff with a guide poling the anglers across a flat in search of fish or staked out in a spot where tarpon are known to pass with regularity. No casting is done until the fish are seen. We would like to emphasize that the Florida Keys boast some of the best shallow-water light-tackle guides in the world. All of them are quite capable of finding tarpon in season and they are skilled at helping you catch them.

You already know that the water temperature on the flats must be 75° or more before tarpon will leave the sanctuary of deeper water. The migratory run starts below Key West and moves up the chain of islands beginning in January or February, when three or four warm days in a row raise the temperature on the flats. Where the fish come from is a mystery and it is even more baffling to speculate on how they know the shallow water is tolerable. They do, however, and anglers must be alert to these conditions.

The main run starts in March most years and later if the weather has been particularly severe. It will last into July. That is not to say you cannot find the odd fish during other times, but the right season makes all the

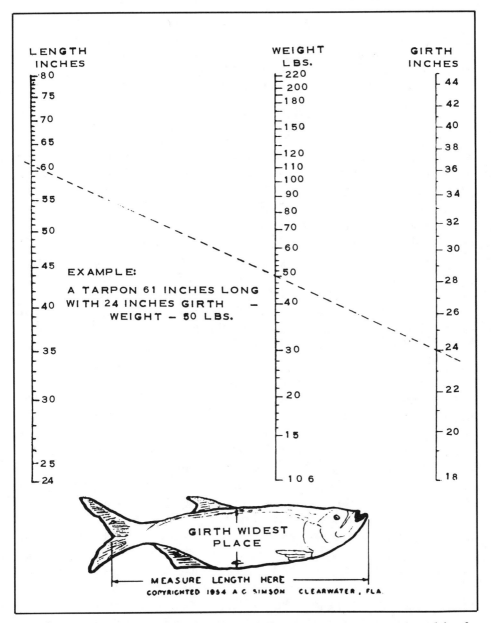

This chart, courtesy of L & S Bait Company, shows how you can estimate the weight of a tarpon by measuring girth and length. It is surprisingly accurate.

difference. On the lower West Coast of Florida, May would have to be the prime month. May and June are the peaks of the season in the Keys. As a basic guideline anywhere within that range, look for the best tarpon fishing in the spring of the year.

Tarpon tend to be slow-growing fish and it probably takes at least a dozen years and possibly more for one to exceed 100 pounds. The largest recorded was a 350-pounder taken in nets off Hillsborough Inlet on Florida's southeast coast. Some exceptionally large fish are now being caught in parts of Africa and there is unexplored tarpon action along the northern coast of Brazil. These places do not offer flats fishing.

A TARPON'S MOUTH

Anyone who has seen a tarpon knows it can open its mouth wide enough to swallow a bowling ball. The inside of that cavern is as hard as a cinder block. Trying to set the hook can present problems for even the most determined fisherman. Unless you take the time to sharpen every hook, the percentage of hookups will drop dramatically. Veterans talk about jumping tarpon rather than landing them because so many fish are able to throw the lure. As they leap clear of the water, these massive fish shake their heads violently from side to side, rattling their gills with bone-jarring authority.

Although tarpon don't have teeth, their mouths are like coarse sandpaper. It is surprising how quickly they can fray through a leader. For that reason, you must use a shock leader of stout monofilament. If you intend to catch fish over 70 pounds, the shock leader should be 90- to 100-pound-test mono. Some anglers use wire, but you will get fewer strikes if you follow their example. For smaller fish, you may scale down the breaking strength of the shock leader accordingly. Along with the shock leader, you must also use a slightly lighter leader long enough to stretch across their backs to prevent fraying of the monofilament. After each fish, check both leaders and change them if they are the least bit worn.

The marvelous thing in hook manufacturing, which relies on a metal stamping machine to fashion the product, is that there is any point at all. Hook makers do an excellent job considering their use of mass production techniques. The points of all hooks, however, should be touched up by hand, especially those used in tarpon fishing.

You can test any hook point by pulling it gently across your thumb nail. If it doesn't dig in immediately, the hook is not sharp enough. Remember that no hook taken directly from the box will do that.

The point is only one consideration. To achieve penetration, a hook must have cutting edges that slice the flesh and push it apart. Hook setting requires that the point hang up momentarily and then the cutting edges take over to insure entry.

There are three basic methods of preparing hooks. The simplest is to lay a file or stone at right angles (first one side and then the other) opposite the barb and just behind the point. If you stroke from the point of the hook back toward the bend, you will not bend the point or curl it. Avoid making a long, tapered point that may collapse when you try to drive it into a fish's mouth. With this method, you have put a cutting edge on the back side of the barb.

The second method is called triangulation, because you actually form three cutting edges in the shape of a triangle. Instead of putting a cutting edge behind the barb as you did in the first method, you file this area flat so that it becomes the base of the triangle. Then, lay the file or stone inside the bend of the hook and file the area flat on either side of the barb from the edge of the base you created to the center of the barb. Each corner of the first flat area has a cutting edge and the third one is right down the center front of the barb.

Finally, you can make a diamond-shaped point. This is a combination of the first two methods. Start as you would in the first technique to create a cutting edge in back of the barb. Then, do the same thing to put a cutting edge on the center front of the barb. If you make the angles correctly, additional cutting edges will be formed halfway between the front and back edges on either side. As you look at the point of the hook, you can actually see a diamond shape with four cutting edges.

Anglers believe that a treble hook or treble-hooked lure has enough barbs to snag anything. Unfortunately, that is not true. Each hook in a treble must be sharpened individually and all trebles on a lure should receive equal attention. We cannot emphasize enough the importance of honing hooks. Your percentage of hookups will soar if you take the time to perform this routine task. In fact, it should be done before you ever leave home. Touchups can be done on the water.

A mill-smooth file will do a good job and there are several makes on the market from which to choose. We use one and believe that it will also work effectively for you.

BAITS AND LURES

Although they may seem so at times, tarpon are not fussy about their general diet. They eat an impressive variety of live and dead baits and may be counted upon to attack an infinite assortment of artificial lures and flies. In fact, light-wand enthusiasts never cease to be amazed at how a tarpon over one hundred pounds will move ten feet out of its way to inhale a skinny streamer that barely spans four inches.

On the flats, live shrimp, crabs, or pinfish make the best baits, but tarpon will also pick up a mullet head lying on the bottom. Purists hate to acknowledge that fact, but it is true and a mullet head in a channel can work wonders.

In casting, live bait holds the edge. The size hook you select depends on the breaking strength of your line, but generally it is better to go with a smaller, light-wire style, because it penetrates more easily. Hook sizes start at about 1/0 and go as high as 6/0 or 7/0 with 20-pound-test line. We recommend a 4/0 hook as standard. You can go up or down from there depending on the situation. Be sure to sharpen the hook.

The larger the shrimp you can find, the easier it will be to cast and the more likely a tarpon will see it. Hook the shrimp through the collar or break the fantail off and thread the hook part way through the body, turning the point so it comes out of the side or the top of the shell.

When you see the tarpon, cast well in front of it, allowing time for the shrimp to settle down to fish eye level. One trick that works well is to overcast the fish and then raise the rod tip slightly as the shrimp strikes the water. This skitters it across the surface, creating a natural sound that will often attract the attention of your quarry.

Tarpon usually swim downtide or downcurrent, so if they don't see the bait, reel in quickly and cast again. They are not about to detect the scent of a shrimp and come back for it as a bonefish might.

Crabs are excellent tarpon bait and are often overlooked by flats fishermen. If you use a crab, remove the claws by crushing them with a pair of pliers. Usually, the crab will throw the claw when you grab it with the pliers. Each end of the carapace has a sharp point or spine. Nip the ends of these with the pliers. The crab should be hooked right near one corner of the carapace with the hook started under the body and exiting through the top of the shell. Be sure to check the hook point after pushing it through the crab.

A live crab will dive for the bottom at the first opportunity, a fact which you can use to your advantage. Cast in front of the fish and keep your rod tip high as you retrieve the live bait across the top of the water. When it is directly in front of the fish, drop the rod tip to create slack line and the crab will swim for cover. As it passes in front of the tarpon, that is the moment of truth.

Live bait fish can be worked with or without a float. Many anglers prefer the float as a means of controlling the depth and keeping the bait from finding a haven in the grass. A piece of styrofoam rigged to break away on the strike makes an excellent float. With a sharp knife, make a slice in opposite sides of the foam and wrap the leader or line around it a couple of times. When the fish hits and the line becomes tight, the monofilament will cut through the foam, releasing it.

It takes fairly stout tackle to cast a pinfish or mullet 35 to 40 feet. As the bait fish strikes the water, it is usually stunned momentarily and struggles to regain its equilibrium. It is then that the tarpon finds it. You do have to cast a considerable distance ahead of your quarry and hope that the fish does not change course. A float may come in handy here, because it does keep the bait at the proper depth and prevents it from seeking the bottom.

It should be noted that pinfish and other live bait are excellent choices for catching tarpon. The silver kings are prowling the flats in search of a meal and will hurriedly swim up to anything that is moving.

A live bait fish should be impaled just in front of the dorsal fin. If the hook is behind the dorsal, the fish will have a tendency to dive. When you push the hook through, be sure a scale does not hang on the point. Otherwise, you will never plant the point in the jaw of a tarpon.

When it comes to artificials, tarpon prefer a lure that moves slowly and hangs almost motionless in the water with only a slight undulating movement. There are times when they will crash an offering, but the typical strike proves disappointing to someone who has never seen it. If the lure is in line

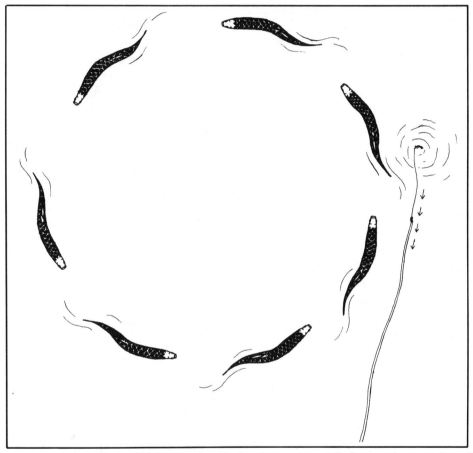

A daisy chain. Some feel it is a courtship display, but no one really knows why a number of tarpon will form a circle and begin swimming directly behind each other. Casting into the center of the circle and retrieving will frighten the fish. Unless you are selecting a special trophy in the daisy chain, it's best to throw to the outside of the chain and retrieve the fly, as shown. This allows a number of fish to look at the fly as they continue circling.

with the direction of the fish, any change of pace is almost imperceptible. The tarpon merely eases ahead, opens its maw, and the lure is gone.

Anglers have searched for a long time for lures that will produce this slight undulating action underwater. Captain Bill Smith developed the forerunner of many modern types by weighting a bullet-shaped cork head and tying hackle to it as though to a fly. By trimming the amount of weight, one could adjust the sink rate and keep the lure at almost neutral buoyancy with very little forward motion. This lure and its modern counterparts are worked by moving the rod slightly to one side and then pausing while recovering slack line. It should be moved as slowly as possible.

When plastic worms became popular for fresh water bass fishing, someone had the idea of using them as a tarpon lure. They work. Some manufacturers make magnum-sized worms that are longer and fatter than the standard ones. They work well in orange, red, or yellow. A slip sinker ahead of the worm will allow you to adjust the weight and sink rate.

Plastics are now available in several different shapes including those that represent bait fish and eels. Any of these are effective. One of the sleepers is the plastic squid in the smaller sizes. It was designed for offshore fishing, but works impressively when cast on a flat. Watch it in the water and you will see that it just hangs there with a slow sink rate. Weight should be added if necessary.

Tarpon will strike a wide range of plugs. The Mirrolure is perhaps the best tarpon plug in use, but you have to give it the correct action. When tarpon are in a channel, our favorite is the green-back Mirrolure 66M18. Cast it in front of the fish, allow it to sink, and work it with very slow and smooth sweeps of the rod, pausing between each one.

Darters are an excellent choice. The yellow darter has long been a good producer on the flats. In fact, most colors work and plugs such as the Mirrolure 88M do a fine job, although they are not known as tarpon producers. Don't overlook the line of Rapalas and Rebels. These baits resemble bait fish and will catch tarpon. Some of the so-called countdown models will drop to fish eye level in a hurry. Those that float, but dive under because of a lip can be worked to tease fish. Simply crank them under, pause—allowing them to rise slightly—and move them again.

Keep in mind that when tarpon are in the shallows, they do not like lures that make a lot of noise. In fact, it may frighten them. A better choice is baits that gurgle gently, but do not pop or chug.

Lead-headed bucktails or those with plastic tails have always caught fish. They can be bounced along the bottom or swept at mid-depth so that they swim. The only problem with the lead-head is that it can be difficult to keep moving right in front of the fish. The weight of the lure also makes it easier for a tarpon to throw it on a jump.

Tarpon will often leave formation and follow a lure right toward the boat. As your heart starts first to flutter and then to pound with the rhythm of native drums, the huge silver beauty seems to hold your offering on the tip of its snout like a sea lion balancing a ball. Anxiously you await the strike, but the fish remains cautious; shortly it will see the boat. When that happens, your only choice is to speed up the retrieve for a short distance. Frequently, this change of pace will provoke the awaited response. If you stop the retrieve, the fish will lose interest immediately.

You must bow to a tarpon—or any jumping fish—and this angler has thrown slack as a baby tarpon of 30 pounds crashes back into the water.

TARPON AND THE FLY ROD

A trout and salmon purist confessed to us recently that if there is such a thing as life after death, he hopes that his assignment will be on a tarpon-filled flat with a fly rod in his hand. To him—and to many of us—that would be the ultimate reward. Anyone who has wrestled a gargantuan silver king into submission with a slender fly rod will never forget the experience and will rightfully count it as a major angling achievement.

The fly rod you select will be primarily a fighting tool, but it also must be capable of delivering the fly to the target. It will probably handle a weight-forward 12-weight or 13-weight line. Fortunately, you do not have to cast all day with it. In fact, a dozen presentations in the course of a day may be more than enough.

Tackle requirements have been outlined earlier, but we do want to make the point again that the guides on the rod must be large enough to let any connections pass through easily. With the exception of the stripping guide,

What it's all about. Here is a nice tarpon well over 100 pounds that took the small fly shown here. This is perhaps the greatest game fish you can catch in shallow water.

which we think should be 16mm in diameter, and a hefty tip top, we use the largest snake guides we can find. The reason is that if a small knot develops, we want it to go through the guides without tearing them off the rod or breaking the leader tippet.

As a basic guideline, you will find that lighter-colored flies are more visible over a dark bottom and vice versa. Almost all tarpon flies are small, measuring from two to four inches. One reason for this is that the average angler finds it easier to cast a small fly. There are times, however, when bigger and bulkier flies that measure five, six, or even seven inches can attract a fish that refuses a smaller fly.

When tarpon are laid up and lying motionless with the tips of their tail and dorsal extended, a longer and bulkier fly has the advantage of sinking more slowly. The trick in this situation is to use a lengthier leader and drop the fly gently on the nose of the fish. If you cast to the side and bring it by the tarpon, your quarry may flush from it.

Tarpon may be finicky on certain days, so it pays to have ready flies in several color combinations. Black is a color that has long been overlooked for tarpon and there are times when an all-black Deceiver is deadly. Bill and Mary Beth Luscombe in DeLand, Florida, tie a significant number of tarpon flies for guides and many of their customers. The Luscombes tell us that the professionals are constantly asking for different color combinations from day to day and week to week. That doesn't mean the basics won't work, but time on the water shows that particular flies catch fish on particular days.

We've already talked about the advantages of looping the leader system directly to the end of the fly line. If you need a longer leader and use a butt section, there should be a loop in the end of it. Class tippet and shock tippet should be tied together in advance using a Bimini Twist, with a double surgeon's loop in the class tippet connecting to the loop in the fly line or butt section. Most guides tie a fly to the end of each leader in advance. Then they merely unloop one and loop on the next one.

Beginners exhibit the tendency to move a fly through the water too fast. The hackle wings breathe in the water and look alive. Instead, the fly should be worked slowly with short swimming strokes. When a fish follows, you can boost the chances of a hookup by watching closely. If you see the tail of the tarpon shake slightly, it is increasing its speed to grab the fly. Instead of continuing to strip line, hesitate for a beat. Usually, the tarpon will open its mouth and overrun the fly, taking it deeper. Do not, however, stop the retrieve at any other time.

In delicate situations when tarpon have appeared suddenly on the flats after a cold snap or when they are over white sand and particularly skittish, you may have to lead the fish more than you would under more typical conditions. There are even situations when you may have to resort to leaders as long as 12 feet or more. This should be evident when the first few fish flush from the presentation.

SMALL TARPON

Baby tarpon weighing up to about 20 pounds and small tarpon up to about 50 pounds are a delight to catch on tackle matched to the task. They are aggressive fish and jump wildly in protest to being hooked, but they can be handled on fairly light gear if you know how to apply the pressure.

These smaller fish are found along the mangrove keys that pockmark the flats, often back under the overhanging branches. They are particularly abundant on the high spring tides of late spring, summer, and early fall, when they lie under the mangroves waiting to ambush their prey. Because they are motionless, anglers tend to mistake them for barracuda. In some places, and especially where there is a deep cut or hole in the bottom, you may find as many as 20 of them together.

Many of the coves and little bays leading off the flats hold tarpon of this size, especially in the Caribbean. You can sometimes see bubbles on the surface marking the spot where they rolled, gulped air, and then let it escape. There are flats in Florida Bay where the smaller tarpon prowl regularly and they are often caught when one is blind casting for a mixed bag.

Tiny darters and other small plugs that do not splash loudly are a perfect choice. Smaller plastic worms and action-tails may also be used. And these fish suck in a shrimp almost as fast as a youngster makes a candy bar disappear.

Nothing surpasses fly fishing for these smaller fish. An 8 or 9 outfit with flies tied on a 1/0 hook is perfect. Fish them as you would giant laid-up fish; drop the fly right in front of them. You may have to tuck it under an overhanging limb to reach them. The strike is often instantaneous.

A silent approach is paramount in this type of fishing. Once the tarpon know you are there, they will move off. On some days, you may see them working their way back under the mangroves where you cannot reach them with a cast, or you may at least suspect that they are there. Some of the Marathon guides have developed a trick worth remembering on such occasions. You only get one shot at the fish, so you had better be ready.

They take the pushpole and slap it down on the water several times, fully extended toward the mangroves. Shortly after that, the fish may start to come out, and that's the time to drop the fly in front of them. Those tarpon want to see what made the commotion. If you hook a fish back in the mangroves and it starts swimming under the limbs, thrust the whole rod in the water much as you would if a fish went under the boat. This keeps the line deeper so that it may clear the branches that touch the surface or dip beneath it.

Whenever you have an opportunity to do this type of fishing, whether for baby tarpon or the giants, don't pass it up. You will never have a more meaningful or memorable angling experience. In fact, as one fellow put it, "I thought I died and went to Heaven."

9 · Bonefish and Permit

BONEFISHING IS ADDICTIVE. THE GRAY GHOST OF THE flats may lack the bulk and brute force of the tarpon, but it makes up for it with a marked degree of wariness. A number of the world's leading anglers rank the bonefish as one of their all-time favorite species.

For the fisherman coming from the trout streams and salmon rivers, the bonefish was made to order. Frequently, the same tackle is acceptable and delicacy of presentation becomes paramount. Since the water ranges from a foot to perhaps three feet, one can easily wade for bonefish providing the bottom is hard enough to support the weight of a human being.

Known as *Albula vulpes*, the bonefish is found in the tropical and subtropical seas of the world. Scientists identify the 20°C. isotherm as the dividing line. We know the threshold better as 68°F. water. Guides may be able to find a fish or two in slightly cooler water, but to catch bonefish consistently, the water temperature must exceed 70°F.

If you study their physical features, you recognize the marks of a fish originally built to feed on the bottom in deep water. They do just that in places such as Hawaii or off Angola in Africa. Where the tidal range is not great and there are expanses of flats, bonefish will come into the shallows to feed. Invariably, the better flats have turtle grass on them or some other form of marine growth. Bonefish often cross white sand flats and may feed in passing, but they seldom stay long. They will, however, sometimes look for food over coral or hard rock flats.

FINDING BONEFISH

Bermuda hosts a few bonefish along the deeper, somewhat sandy flats during the summer months and seems to be the northern extent of their range. In the United States, Biscayne Bay marks the upper limit and some of the

A bonefish may have an inferior mouth on the underside of its snout, but its eyes are large and well-equipped to spot even the tiniest prey. This fish took a small fly inched along the bottom.

largest fish are taken from these waters. From Key Biscayne through Key Largo, Islamorada, and Marathon, bonefishing is excellent. There are some good places farther down in the Keys, but by the time one reaches Key West, the bonefish have virtually disappeared. The flats look the same to our untrained eyes, but finding bonefish is a phenomenon.

They do inhabit many of the flats fed by the Gulf of Mexico all the way down into the Lower Keys and past the Contents and Sawyer Keys. In Florida Bay, you may locate some fish as far as Nine Mile Bank, but bonefish are not caught in Flamingo very often. There are, however, a few banks near Flamingo where some of the largest bonefish in Florida are taken each year. The Bahamas, of course, have some choice spots, including the Deep Water Cay area and throughout the island chain. Bonefish are plentiful in parts of Mexico's Yucatan and through Belize. There is even the odd one in the shallows of Southern California's Newport Bay.

After an extensive study, Gerard Bruger of the Florida Department of Natural Resources notes that three-quarters of the typical bonefish diet consists of shrimp, crabs, and other crustaceans. Small fish and mollusks make up most of the balance. These facts can be interpreted to mean that bonefish are constantly searching the bottom for their food. In fact, their mouths, which are considered inferior by scientists, are located on the underside of the head so the fish can dip down and pick up food.

Despite the general insistence that the first of the rising tide is prime time for bonefish, there is in fact no single best stage of the water. Optimal tidal conditions depend on the type of flat, its location, where on the flat you are fishing, and so forth. What the specialists are really saying is that you can start at low slack water and follow the cycle of the tide through the rise and fall if you don't know the area. To do this effectively, one must find an ocean or gulf flat. Usually, the fish will come out of the deep water as the tide starts in.

Never lose sight of the fact that there are places that produce fish on incoming tide and those that become active when the water turns out. Captain Frank Garisto, who works Biscayne Bay, talks about days when the fishing is good on one tide and poor on another, even though he has spots tailored to every stage. Part of the fun of bonefishing is in trying to figure out where the fish will be and when.

TACKLE AND TECHNIQUES

More bonefish are taken on light spinning tackle than on all other types combined. The main reason is the need to cast light lures or shrimp, which is difficult to do with plug gear. Lines testing eight or ten pounds are about average. Some veterans opt for lighter lines, but they are not necessary to catch fish.

If you are fishing with artificial lures, you may want a short shock leader of perhaps 20-pound-test line as protection against fraying. It also helps if you toss the lure to some other species. Bait fishermen often employ shock leaders, but in some areas the trend is away from this. Guides simply double the line and tie it directly to the hook.

You already know that bonefish generally feed into the tide or current and that their sense of smell plays an important role in aiding them to find food. They expect their meals to be swept along with the tide or to come down to them from the upcurrent side. A presentation from this direction is there-fore more effective.

Live shrimp are the basic bonefish bait. Cut off the fantail and thread a 1/0 or 2/0 hook through the shrimp, starting at the tail. Bring the point out through the side or back of the shell. Threading the hook in this way makes it more difficult for the shrimp to be cast off during the presentation. As you stand on the casting platform with bail open, remember to keep the shrimp in the water so that it stays alive.

Once you see the fish, cast the shrimp 10 to 12 feet in front of it and across its path. Then, lift the rod tip and skitter the shrimp along the surface until it is opposite the bonefish. If you made the cast uptide, the gray ghost will hear and smell the offering and should be onto it quickly. Even if the shrimp goes into the grass, a bonefish can ferret it out. Moving the shrimp suddenly when the fish is nearby may spook your quarry.

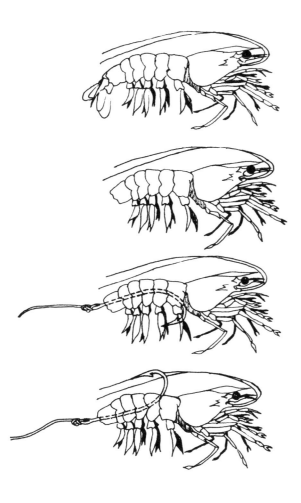

Most anglers don't realize that there is a better way to hook a shrimp. The top shows a shrimp; the drawing beneath it shows the tail section removed so it will move through the water better. Third from top shows how most people rig a shrimp, with the hook coming out of the soft belly. Several casts, and the bait usually slips down on the hook. The bottom drawing shows that bringing the hook out of the upper back, where the shell is firm, gives the hook the best grip for casting.

Casting a shrimp without additional weight takes a bit of practice. Some specialists use longer rods (up to 8½ feet,), but a 6½- to 7½-foot rod should prove adequate. If the current is strong and the fish are near the bottom, you can add a tiny split-shot sinker or two in front of the shrimp. This will help to get it down.

Flies and lures for bonefishing have traditionally been small because the mouth of a bonefish is not exceptionally large. Lead-headed bucktails or those with plastic tails have long been the accepted choice for catching bonefish. Weights vary from one-eighth ounce to one-quarter ounce. Use the lightest lure you can based on your ability to cast it and get it in front of the fish. Lighter lures enter the water with less commotion and can be cast closer to the fish.

The major problem in bonefishing is to put a bait or lure where the fish can see it without alarming your quarry. It isn't easy. To compound matters,

Some of the most effective spinning lures for bonefish. Top row, left to right: 1/16-ounce jig head with plastic action-tail (usually best are orange, red or chartruse); Burke's 4-inch Hook Worm; in root-beer color it is judged by many guides as one of the best artificial lures you can throw to bones. It can be fished Texas bass-rigged style, with hook buried in the worm and a sliding sinker in front, or as shown without the sinker.

Bottom row, left to right: Bonefish Demon jig by Arbogast, one of many home-made skimmer type jigs with upturned front so it can be hopped along bottom and Nicklelure's Popeye jig.

bonefish never seem to follow the same course for more than ten feet and you can be sure they will change direction the instant you release the cast. When that happens, reel in as fast as you can and make another presentation.

Most bonefish jigs have a flat bottom so that the hook rides in a turned-up position and does not hang in the grass. This design also looks to the bonefish as if it is trying to burrow in the sand, since the tail sticks up. Other bucktail shapes can be used where there is less grass. The basic retrieve should involve minor movement on the bottom. You have merely to "kick" a bucktail by flicking the rod tip, for bonefish are very alert to movement. The tiny puff of sand or marl released when the lead-head bounces is all it takes to attract the fish. Forward motion should be minimized as long as the lure shows that it's "alive."

Henry Ford may have preferred black automobiles, but bonefish show a preference for brown lures. If you are in doubt, make brown your first choice,

The two artificial lures that have taken the most permit are the Popeye jig (usually in a sand color) and the Puff, originated by Captain Nat Ragland of Marathon, and used by many anglers. This pattern was tied by Chico Fernandez.

white your second. In fact, our strategy has always been one of contrasts. Start with a dark lure and, if it is refused, switch immediately to a light color. The reverse is also true. If a white or yellow or pink offering is turned down, try darker colors. You might have to switch back and forth throughout the day.

Not many people realize that bonefish will sometimes strike a jig that is moved at maximum speed. Stu Apte was the first to show us that back in the days when he was guiding in the Florida Keys. Whenever a school of bonefish was spooked, he would make a long cast in front of them and retrieve the jig using a Florida whip, which is nothing more than jigging horizontally and reeling as fast as possible. Once in a while, a bonefish would put on the brakes or detour for an instant to grab the lure. It is worth a shot since the fish are spooked anyway. Barracuda sometimes grab a lure retrieved at that speed, so a short piece of number two wire is advisable.

For years it was believed that bonefish could only be taken on a pink shrimp fly tied on a 1/0 hook. That thinking has changed in terms of color, hook size, and materials. The majority of shrimp on a flat are translucent, so fly tiers have gone to materials such as Fishair or acrylic yarns. Noted tier Chico Fernandez of Miami likes to put a grizzly wing on either side, pointing out that it adds a realistic touch by imitating the innards of a cracking shrimp, a favorite food, or of a small bait fish.

Five methods of tying a cracking shrimp (popular bonefish pattern) fly. Top, left to right: reverse tied wing and conventional tie. Lower row, left to right: smallest bead chain eyes available, mounted on bottom of lure to insure that it falls properly; reverse tie with a mono loop and the same fly tied on a Keel hook.

Bart Foth has caught more trophy bonefish on fly than anyone. In the mid-1960s, he discovered that these fish would take a fly tied on a #6, #4 or #2 hook more readily than one tied on a larger hook. He felt that the big advantage lay in the relative ease of putting the smaller fly close to the fish without spooking it. This is particularly true with tailing bonefish.

Long strips or sweeps of a fly will frighten bonefish. The correct retrieve is to move the fly an inch or so at a time by barely ticking the fly line. In some

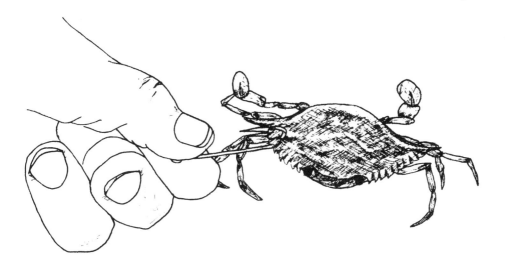

Small crabs make good bonefish baits, and silver-dollar-size ones are the best bait for permit. Best hooking method is to remove the claws, then carefully hook the crab through one of the outer points. Be sure hook point wasn't dulled by this operation. On some larger crabs, many guides prefer to break off the sharp points.

cases, the fly will swim in the current and the wing materials will breathe. That is often all it takes. If you tie your own flies, you may want to add some weight to the head so that they dive more quickly. On deeper flats and when the current is strong, you may need the weight to get the offering down to the level of the fish.

If you happen to be fishing bones in very skinny water, switch to flies that are bulkier and have more wing material. They will suspend better and will not hang in the grass. A number of bonefish patterns are tied on keel hooks to make them weedless, which may be important on some flats. Most tiers also use a reverse tie so that the dressing covers the point of the hook. One of the most effective flies we have seen is tied by Bill and Mary Beth Luscombe of DeLand. They use a tiny drop of solder behind the eye of the hook to make the fly stand upright.

If you watch a bonefish, you can usually tell when it has seen a lure or fly. The tail seems to pulsate with excitement and its body shakes. The fish concentrates on what it thinks is a meal and either follows it or strikes immediately. If he follows, you merely have to "kick" the lure in place and the fish should pounce on it.

Few anglers use crabs as bonefish bait, probably because they are more difficult to obtain. However, you should know that they work very well. Tiny white ghost crabs are an excellent bait and so are other species that are about the size of a quarter or a Susan B. Anthony dollar.

Bonefish are bottom feeders, and often will stand on their noses to root out a morsel hiding in the bottom. Permit and redfish will do the same thing. Here a bonefish's tail protrudes above the surface as it seeks something in the grass.

TAILING FISH

No sight is more thrilling than the silver tails of bonefish twitching and flashing like signal mirrors in the brilliant sun. The panorama before you includes tiny puffs of marl escaping from the bottom as a gray ghost roots for a burrowing goodie. The shallowness of the water increases the excitement. In some places, it is impossible to get the boat to the fish and you must step over the side and wade. On foot or by boat, the approach is critical.

Timing and accuracy make the difference in this phase of bonefishing. When a fish has its head down and tail up, you can drop a bait, lure, or fly closer than you can when the fish is simply swimming. Usually, several fish are tailing together, so it becomes a matter of picking the fish and being careful not to let the line come too close to the others in the school.

A shrimp can be presented closer to a tailing bonefish than anything else. It has a natural sound when it hits the water and can be dropped within a few feet. Then, when the fish lifts its head, the natural is right there. With bait, cast on the upcurrent side so that the scent filters down to the fish. If the fish moves off, recover the shrimp quickly and cast again. Don't wait a long time for the fish to find it.

Fly fishermen have the advantage in this situation over those who use other casting gear with artificial lures. Using a nine to twelve-foot leader, you can put a fly within a foot or two of the fish. The key lies in using full-bodied patterns that parachute to the water and don't sink very fast. As the fish looks up, you have merely to twitch the fly once or twice for it to be seen.

If you take the time to make a couple of false casts, you can dry the fly and it will drop to the water more gently than a water-soaked version. Those false casts, by the way, must be made in another direction. A line in the air over the fish is enough to spook them or at least make them wary. White fly lines, which are highly visible, are particularly poor choices for that reason. Once a bonefish is alerted, he is difficult to fool.

Plastic bait tails or worms weighted with tiny split shot can be cast closer to the fish than the heavier lead-headed jigs. If you do use a jig, cast a comfortable distance from the target area. Then, bounce the lure back into the vicinity of the fish so that they think they rooted it out while they were nose-diving for something else. One trick that works well is to overcast the spot you want to hit, stop the lure in mid-air, and start the retrieve before the artificial strikes the water. That causes the lure to angle back and it cuts

This angler is demonstrating the wrong way to wade a flat. Stingrays hide beneath a layer of mud and stepping on a stingray can mean problems. But if you drag your toe forward, keeping it in contact with the bottom, you will touch the ray, instead of stepping on it—and the ray flees without harm to you or it. Always wade flats by dragging the foot forward.

across the surface rather than dropping loudly on it. You will also find that jigs with slightly curved bases enter the water more silently than those with perfectly flat bottoms.

When the water depth is 15 inches or less, there's an excellent chance to see tailing bonefish. Be sure to scan the surface of the water periodically and look for tails or wakes. You should still check out the bottom, but switch your search pattern back and forth in skinny water.

CHUMMING

Under the right tidal and wind conditions, bonefish can pick up the scent of shrimp, crabs, or conch as far away as 100 yards. Chumming has proved to be an exciting technique for tolling bonefish within casting range. Captain J. T. Harrod, fishing out of Miami's famous Pier 5 in the 1940s from a skiff powered by a pair of 25-horsepower outboards—the ultimate in engines in those days—used the method in Biscayne Bay. Captain Bill Curtis picked up where Harrod left off with exceptional success. Later, Captain Frank Garisto began guiding in Biscayne Bay and both men still produce an incredible number of bonefish for their clients using this system, working the flats from Key Biscayne to Key Largo.

A bonefish being released. We must release them if we want to keep fishing for this great trophy. Spinning lines testing 6 to 8 pounds are ideal for this fish.

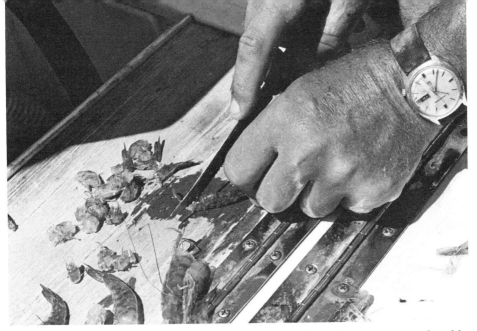

One of the most deadly methods of catching bonefish is to chum them, a system perfected by Captain Bill Curtis. The shrimp are cut into half-inch sections.

With some basic knowledge, almost anyone can chum. The idea is to pick a flat on which bonefish feed or cross at a particular stage of the tide. If possible, the sun should be at your back and you should be upcurrent from where the chum lies. To make it easier to see the fish, pick a white-sand spot or light-colored bottom.

Your guide will first test your ability to cast and then position the boat so that you can reach the fish without straining. Of course, the boat has to be far enough away so as not to spook the bonefish. On a soft bottom, a pushpole is inserted in the marl and the boat tied to it. An anchor is used over rocky terrain.

Once the boat is staked out, the guide cuts about ten shrimp into pieces the size of a fingernail. He tosses this handful so that the pieces land in the light-colored spot previously picked. Then, he baits your hook with a live shrimp (tail removed) and both of you watch the spot where the shrimp lie on the bottom. You can see the bonefish as they enter the area and start to search for the food. That's when you drop a shrimp in front of the fish and you should have a pickup.

If you prefer it to live bait, you can use artificial lures or a fly rod for the cast. The idea is to bring the bonefish within casting range. Once they are there, you fish them just as you would any other bonefish. It is an easier task for the fly fisherman. He can measure the distance in advance and have just the right amount of line stripped off the reel. Fly patterns that undulate particularly well should be used so that, after the cast is made, the fly hangs in the current breathing. The bonefish are moving back and forth in a concentrated area looking for scraps of shrimp, so there's a good chance they will see the offering. Should they hesitate in picking it up, cast again.

Veteran chummers often set up shop high on a flat, because experience has taught them the best places. However, this method can also be effective relatively close to deeper water. The scent of the shrimp will move over the edge and actually pull fish up on the flat to investigate. On an outgoing tide, you should be inside the far edge of the flat. When the tide is flooding, your position is closer to the place where they would enter the flat.

In the Bahamas, native guides have been chumming with cut up pieces of conch for a long time. They even bait the hook with a juicy segment of this tasty offering and let it sit on the bottom amidst the chum. They do not attempt to spot the fish first, often preferring to do the chumming in deeper water or where turbidity is a problem.

THE ELUSIVE PERMIT

Most people have never heard of a permit, much less caught one. They are one of the prizes of flats fishing and a particularly difficult species to locate and catch. Permit are not as abundant as bonefish and they never seem to stop moving. If you think the gray ghost is skittish, try fishing for permit. They are seldom around long enough for a good presentation. When you have a shot, you must be on target or the fish are gone. Often a guide will point to a departing fish and announce "that was a permit."

A deep-bodied fish, the permit has the battle instinct and tenacity of a jack crevalle and the wariness of a bonefish. At times, the jack in them comes out and they'll clobber anything. There are other days when they ignore everything.

A permit in very shallow water with both dorsal and tail fin exposed. Under such conditions it is even more difficult to approach them and to cast without frightening them.

Opposite: A 32-pound permit on 8-pound test—it took better than half an hour to subdue the trophy, which was released.

Because of their girth, permit require deeper water and you will seldom find them in less than 18 inches. They stay a lot deeper on the flat, preferring to feed along the outside edges where water depth may be three to five feet or more. Usually, they come onto the flats later on the tide than bonefish. One reason that bonefishermen do not see permit very often is that they are usually fishing in too shallow water. The mirror reflections from the silver sides of the fish leave nothing but a bit of black on dorsal and tail. There are places west of Key West and in the Gulf such as the Contents and Sawyers where permit are plentiful at certain times of the year. The peak seasons are spring and fall.

Permit seem to prefer rocky or coral bottoms, primarily because they feed on crabs or bait fish and tend to find more over these surfaces. You will also find them patrolling back and forth where miniature rock formations cause the tide to tumble and disorient the bait. Although they are found on inside flats, most of them remain fairly close to the ocean or gulf and deep water.

Since they appear without warning and are gone just as quickly, you usually only have one chance to cast whatever bait or lure happens to be in your hand. A surprising number of permit are caught by bonefish or tarpon enthusiasts who simply cast. If you have a choice, a crab about the size of an old silver dollar is perfect. Remove the claws and points on the edge of the carapace just as you would for tarpon. Hook the crab in one corner, bringing the point of the hook from the underside of the crab through the top.

When a permit is spotted, cast the crab well beyond the fish and hold the rod tip high to keep the crustacean on top of the water. Reel steadily and actually swim the crab across the water. The permit will spot it and you will see the swirl as the fish races for its victim. As soon as you detect any movement other than normal swimming on the part of the permit, drop the rod tip and stop reeling. At the same time, open the bail on the spinning outfit or put the plug reel in freespool.

The crab will dive for the bottom as soon as it feels the slack line and the permit should be in hot pursuit. Wait a couple of seconds, close the bail, and when the line becomes tight, set the hook. A live shrimp can be worked in similar fashion, although when the shrimp is in front of the fish, it pays to let it sink under the surface whether the permit has seen it or not.

The best permit lure is a sand-colored jig weighing about three-eighths of an ounce, although the fish will hit a variety of artificials. They will sometimes chase tube lures tailored for barracuda and they have been known to hit plugs, plastic worms, and virtually anything else used for tarpon or bonefish.

Catching one on fly is a supreme angling challenge. Not many people have done it at all and there are only a few men who have caught a respectable number. If there is such a thing as a permit fly, it would have to be Captain Nat Ragland's Puff Fly which has accounted for more permit than any other pattern. No one can really tell why a permit hits a fly. You can make a thousand casts to the fish and get a turn-down on every one. Then, you make another cast and the permit charges it like a cavalryman.

Under certain conditions, permit have a habit of laying up just like tarpon. They will remain motionless just under the surface with their tail and dorsal showing, sometimes looking like the tips of twigs. You can sometimes make them take a fly by casting a muddler or streamer pattern that will remain close to the surface. The key is to cast to one side and let the current carry the fly to the fish. If you do it right, the streamer will sweep broadside of the fish and the permit will take.

There are rare occasions when you see permit tailing just like bonefish. If you get close enough for a cast, put the fly, lure, or bait much closer than you would if the fish were free-swimming. You want it to look up and suddenly to see your offering in front of it. That is always a good way to catch a fish, because it then strikes out of instinct and without consideration.

Catching a tarpon, bonefish, and permit on the flats in a single day is considered a grand slam and quite an angling achievement. Usually, the person first catches the permit and then the tarpon and bonefish. You may have the tarpon and bonefish, but that doesn't mean you have a chance at the permit. Maddening elusiveness is what permit fishing is all about. Once you land one, however, you'll know you have a treasure.

10 · Barracuda and Sharks

Barracuda and sharks have been maligned by anglers and guides who seek the more glamorous denizens of the shallow flats. They are usually relegated to the second-class role reserved for the so-called "day-savers" that one hopes to catch when all else fails. To our way of thinking, that's a mistake. These toothy critters are underrated in skinny water. Not only are they tough to fool, but they put up spectacular battles complete with sizzling runs that leave a bonefish gasping in the shallows.

Small specimens of both species seem to be on the flats most of the time. As we pointed out earlier, we like to see plenty of sharks and barracuda on the flats when we are bonefishing, for it is a sign that at least some moderate-sized bonefish are there, too. Of course, if you wish to tangle with trophy-sized fish, you must time the season closely.

Sharks prefer warm weather and you will find consistently larger ones on the flats during the summer months than at other times. That is not to say that you won't find six- or even eight-footers in the winter, but there are not as many and they are prone to leave when water temperatures fluctuate. March and April are excellent times around Key West for really big sharks.

Big barracuda invade the flats when the weather turns cold and water temperature drops as though drawn by an unseen hand. You will find them in January, February, and March, particularly during the cold snaps that send bonefish and permit scurrying for the comfort of deeper water. Some of these fish look like logs in the water with dentures that resemble the blade of a buzzsaw.

Bermuda boasts an abundance of barracuda during the summer months, but the water temperature inshore is not as hot as it is in Florida. There are times when the saber-toothed barracuda lies motionless on the surface and there are fish at every point on the compass. The barracuda provides a challenge throughout the Caribbean in channels, on the flats, and along the edges. Because water temperatures are more moderate there, sharks and barracuda may be found during most of the year.

FISHING FOR BARRACUDA

There is no question that the surgical tube lure is the bane of barracuda. Although it functions as an illusion in the water, it triggers a 'cuda to strike faster than anything else. The tubing imitates a needlefish and appears to be snaking its way through the water, though it is in fact spinning.

Not everyone has the same view on how to work tube lures in the water. Captain John Eckard of Key West, Florida, has been making tubes for years and has developed a veritable fish-catching formula—which we'll share with you in a moment. He has always insisted that if you work the lure just beneath the surface of the water, it will attract more barracuda. Captain Harry Spear of Marathon disagrees. Harry is adamant about dancing the lure on the surface and never letting it dip beneath.

On two successive days, we fished with John and then with Harry, working waters in the backcountry of the Lower Keys that were only a couple of miles apart. We are pleased to report that both methods produced barracuda with equal effectiveness.

Almost all of the commercially available surgical tubes range from 10 to 12 inches in length. It is easy to make your own and we feel that John Eckard's design is as good as anything we have seen. He uses tubes that are 15 to 18 inches in length with chartreuse the number one color, followed by fluorescent red, natural, and black.

A tube should be rigged with a belly hook and a 3/0 to 5/0 tail hook. Whether you use trebles or single hooks is a personal choice. You will need an egg sinker or slip sinker weighing between one-quarter and one-half ounce and stainless steel wire in # 6, 7, or 8. The tubing should always be kept coiled so that it retains its natural curvature, both before you make the rigs and after they are completed.

According to John, the belly hook must be above the center of the tubing. If you have a sixteen-inch tube, the belly hook should be less than eight inches from the head. You'll miss fewer fish with that positioning. Wire each hook separately, cutting a hole in the tube for the belly hook and pushing both wires through the front end of the tube. Slip the sinker over both wires and secure it with a twisted loop. You may use a swivel or a split ring in front of the sinker as a connector.

Standard tubing has a three-eighths-inch O.D. If you prefer using lighter lines such as four- six- or eight-pound-test, you must use thinner and shorter tubes. The diameter should be one-eighth to three-sixteenths inches, and the overall length about twelve inches. Hook sizes should be correspondingly smaller.

Over a sandy bottom, barracuda seem to take on a lighter color to blend with their surroundings. This big critter held by a Bahamian guide ran down a fast-moving tube lure.

We tie a heavy monofilament leader directly to the swivel or split ring and find we get more strikes. Although double-hook tube lures miss fewer strikes, they also have a disadvantage. Since the tubing is curved, the line sometimes catches on the center hook and destroys the action—a fact worth thinking about when you decide how to rig.

Barracuda are exceptionally wary fish and often refuse to strike once they have seen you or the boat. They are also skittish and if the lure lands too close to them or angles toward them in an attacking attitude, you can bet they will flee. Therefore, you must make very long casts. Aim the lure at a spot to one side of the barracuda and beyond it.

The retrieve should start with one or two short jerks and then take off at flank speed. Try to buzz that lure right back to the boat. The 'cuda will chase it from an incredible distance and the strike is so fast that you will never see it. Usually, the water bulges and it looks as if a torpedo is heading directly for the tube. You wonder whether the barracuda will grab the lure before it sees the boat. If the tube begins to get too close, stop it momentarily, let it sink, and twitch it once or twice. If that doesn't work, start cranking again.

A word or caution: always shift the rod to one side as the lure approaches the boat. Barracuda have been known to clear the water in an attempt to grab the lure just as the angler is lifting it to make another cast. A rod pointed at the lure brings the fish directly at your face.

Obviously, spinning tackle is the first choice for barracuda fishing because it has a faster rate of retrieve than plug gear. It is also a lot easier to cast a long tube lure with spinning than with other tackle.

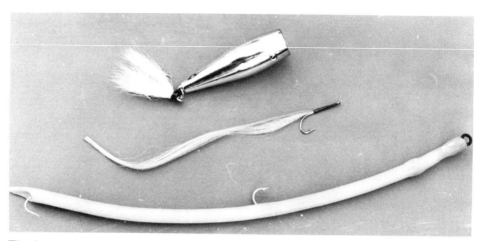

The three dependable lures for barracuda, top to bottom: Chugger, a scoop-faced noisy plug that can be retrieved rapidly or with long sweeps of the rod to give off loud popping sounds. Cuda fly, made from 10-inch-long FisHair. It is often dressed with white belly, light green midwing and top wing of either dark blue or green to imitate a needlefish. It is also effective in bright orange or red. At bottom is the famed tube lure, made from plastic tubing—see instructions in text for how to make it.

If you don't have a tube lure, substitute a plastic worm with a slip sinker. The problem here, however, is that the cuda will chop the worm in two on the first strike and you will have to keep replacing it. In fact, when a tube lure has been slashed up and you have experienced a few refusals, change to a new one. You will find that barracuda have tremendous eyesight and will turn away from anything that looks unusual.

Experienced anglers often throw darter-type plugs to barracuda, and they do quite well with stick baits that dance across the surface. With the darters, they employ a slow and tantalizing retrieve, while the stick baits are walked quickly across the surface.

The fly fisherman had problems in the past getting a barracuda to strike. When he wanted one to take a fly, it wouldn't; but when he cast to a tarpon, the 'cuda darted in front of the silver king and stole the hunk of feathers or hair. That scenario changed a few years back when Ray Donnersberger and George Cornish started fishing with an extremely long fly made from Fishair. It has become the standard fly for barracuda, undulating through the water like a tube lure. Because it is so long—sometimes nine or ten inches—and snakes across the top, it can be retrieved more slowly and still elicit a positive response.

To fish 'cuda with fly, you should use a very short section—about three or four inches—of single-strand, stainless steel wire between the fly and the rest of the shock leader or tippet. Fishair comes in a variety of colors and densities and we use it in fly patterns for barracuda, bonefish, and many other species. On a long barracuda fly, glue the rear of the Fishair together to prevent it from blossoming out each time the fly pulses in the water. Gluing will also make the fly cast more easily.

Another method of fly fishing a barracuda depends more on opportunity than anything else. Occasionally this predator will chop a fish in half right next to the boat. When that happens, you can toss a white or silver fly into the water and let the current drift it back without any movement. The barracuda sees it as another piece of the fish he just sampled and often comes back to pick it up.

Whenever the boat is close to a channel or a white sand patch, it pays to make a few blind casts for barracuda. Toss out a tube lure, fly, or plug and work it back to the boat. If there is a barracuda around, chances are that it will charge the offering and you are then in for some exciting sport.

This angler waded near the dark channel in front of him and hooked a huge cuda. Cudas on flats tend to lie in ambush either in pockets or holes on the flats, or along the channel edge bordering a flat.

Lefty Kreh with a nice cuda that took a FisHair streamer fly.

JOUSTING WITH JAWS

With dorsal fin extended like a sail and tail beating back and forth with the cadence of a metronome, a shark will knife its way through extremely shallow water searching for an easy meal. They are nature's most successful predator, having existed in the same basic form for eons. When you see them on a flat, you know that there are other fish about. Some of these sharks are big enough to send a shiver down your spine and make you glad you're aboard a boat.

In spite of their ferocious jaws, sandpaper hide, and aggressive appearance, sharks are among the most skittish fish in shallow water. A seven-footer will flee in panic if a quarter-ounce bucktail lands too close or a heavy flyline startles it. They demand a stealthy approach. There are plenty of small bonnet sharks on the flats, as well as blacktips, lemons, an occasional bull, and a few other species. Nurse sharks are present, but they seldom take a lure. And if they do, they tend to fight poorly.

The most important thing to remember about sharks is that they can cover a lot of territory in a hurry. You may spot one in the distance and think you have plenty of time to get ready. Often, you continue looking for bonefish or tarpon, figuring that you will check on the shark in a few minutes. In a fraction of that time, the shark is suddenly near the boat. On the other hand, you should also recognize that poling after one is not easy.

Since the clarity of the eyesight of a shark is unknown—although scientists are beginning to believe it is better than we once thought—it is best to appeal to its sense of smell. Smaller sharks will find a shrimp or piece of bait if it is cast near them and slightly uptide. They are fun to catch on light outfits and an ideal adversary for youngsters. If you have a live shrimp, cast it alongside one eye and move it until you get the shark's attention. Then drop the bait and the shark will find it.

Balao is the answer for bigger sharks. A whole balao has enough weight to be cast easily and can be dragged across the surface like an artificial lure. You simply hook the balao through the head with the hook going from bottom to top. The idea is to fish it as an artificial, but use the natural bait properties. When you spot a shark, make a cast across the path of the shark or down along one side. Keep the rod high and reel the balao right across the top of the water. As the shark goes for it, drop the rod and let it settle. Even if the fish misses the bait, it will circle and pick it up. There is no better system.

People view sharks as feeding machines, assuming that they will attack anything they see or hear. If you believe that, try catching one on an artificial lure. Most of the time you will come away frustrated by the refusals. On the other hand, sharks are unpredictable. We have seen the times when we cast to a half-dozen or more in a row and they wouldn't even look at the offering. The next brute coming down the flat attacked the lure with a vengeance.

If you had to choose a single lure, it would have to be a darter. Both the solid types and the model 88 and 99 Mirrolures with plastic V-lips work. Remember that the maw of a shark gets in the way of its vision. The eyes are small and set well back on the head, so the perfect presentation is a long cast down one side of the fish. Work the lure at right angles to the eye and not very far away.

Too much noise will scare a shark. The proper action includes twitches and gurgles and draws the darter just under the surface before letting it come back up. You do not want a fast retrieve. The secret is to keep the darter in the vicinity of the shark for as long as possible. When the shark turns on it, pause until the fish has the lure. Because its mouth is on the underside, the shark sometimes has difficulty closing on the lure.

Lures other than darters also catch sharks. Pencil-popper designs that walk across the water bring strikes. Plastic squids such as Squirt Squid are effective, and you may certainly use the minnow-type plugs such as Rebels and Rapalas. To catch sharks consistently, you should use a foot to about 18 inches of wire leader followed by fairly heavy monofilament. The skin of a shark makes sandpaper look smooth and unless you protect the light line, a shark will fray through it in an instant. When you fight the fish, it's a good idea to keep the line on the same side as the lure so that it doesn't cut across the animal's back.

Anglers who have tried it sing the praises of catching a big shark on fly. It is a challenge from both the standpoint of getting the fish to strike and of weathering the long, long runs at top speed. You will need stout tackle just as you would for tarpon. The flies should be tied on 4/0 or 5/0 hooks so that you can get them around the jaw. Shark flies often have Mylar to add flash and are tied from materials such as polar-bear imitations of long FisHair. Bright hackles in red, orange, yellow, or combinations are tied in at the head so that the angler can see the fly easily and know where it is in relation to the shark. Popping bugs are a poor choice, because sharks inadvertently push them out of the way with their snouts as they try to grab them.

As with the darter, the best presentation is alongside the eye of the fish and the strip retrieve should be slow. The shark must see the fly and turn on it. Once a shark makes up its mind to strike, the action is like stored lightning. Those jaws whip around and the fly is gone if the fish is on-target. Since the shark may swallow the fly, the whole shock tippet should be of single-strand, stainless-steel wire.

Another way to get a cast to a shark involves the use of a dead fish. This method is particularly effective in turbid waters such as you find in Florida Bay around Flamingo. Norman Jansik of Miami was one of the first to use this system and it works. He tows a whole fish behind the boat on a stout line while he fishes for other species. The shark outfit is rigged, ready, and lying within grasp.

When a shark finds the dead fish and starts to feed on it, Norman simply pulls it out of the way and casts a lure or fly to the spot. The shark is busy searching for its meal and has already been turned on by the teaser. If the lure is seen, it usually is struck. Should the shark ignore the lure, the teaser is put back into the water and further efforts are made to excite the critter.

Sharks are curious animals and will move to investigate any disturbance or vibration. If a shark starts to swim off, you can swish your rod tip in the water, creating noise and bubbles. Surprisingly, sharks wil sometimes circle a few times to figure out what's causing those vibrations and that can provide the extra time to get off another cast or two.

A WORD OF CAUTION

The skeleton of a shark is made from cartilage rather than bone as with other species of fish. It is as supple as a garden hose and can turn around and bite its own tail if it so desires. Unless you hold a shark properly, it will whip back and bite you without warning. Wear gloves when you deal with a shark because the skin is so rough. Hold smaller ones behind the head if you must handle them. Larger ones should not be handled at all unless it is absolutely necessary.

Do not put a shark in the boat with you, particularly a big one. *There is no such thing as a dead shark.* The number of sharks that have suddenly come back to life is legendary. Fly rod specialist Bart Foth once had a record shark in the boat that he was bringing in to be weighed. It had been beaten, clubbed, dragged backward, kept out of water for a considerable period and appeared

There's no sense in gaffing and killing a barracuda just to get your lure back. They can be lip-hooked, as shown here, the lure removed with a pair of pliers, and the fish released unharmed.

to be dead. Without warning, it snapped its jaws, bit one of the chairs in the boat, and took a U-shaped piece out of it with the same ease that you would bite into a piece of toast.

Some anglers feel it is macho to kill every shark and barracuda they catch. Actually, both of these species are very vulnerable to fishing pressure and should be released unharmed unless there is a good reason to keep them. A barracuda can be netted and handled easily unless it is large. In the latter case, you might have to slip a release gaff through its lower jaw. Putting a gaff into the body either kills the fish or seriously injures it.

Sharks can be lip-gaffed if necessary, but it makes a lot more sense to sacrifice the lure and turn the animal loose. The same can be done with big barracuda. Anyone who has fished an area such as the Florida Keys over the last half-century can tell you first-hand about the reduction in size over the years of the average shark and barracuda. These are aggressive fish and the bigger ones can be wiped out easily.

11 · The Fun Fish

Bonefish and tarpon capture the headlines and the publicity, but the spotted seatrout still ranks as the most popular shallow water fish from Texas to Florida. Redfish have an impressive following in the same waters. A small cadre of anglers devote every free moment to following the movements of the snook both on the flats and around the oyster bars.

All of this fishing is available to almost everyone. In many coastal areas, one can wade the flats and catch trout and redfish. Other places may require a boat, but they can be reached in everything from an aluminim skiff to a sophisticated puddle jumper.

These species are not as hard to catch as the armor-plated tarpon or the speedy bonefish. Lighter tackle is the order of the day and everyone can have fun catching these less glamorous denizens of shallow waters. They provide an excellent way to teach youngsters the sport and, since these fish are delicious, one can gather the makings of a tasty dinner.

In certain areas trout, snook, and redfish populations have declined in recent years. Loss of habitat has been a major factor, but one cannot overlook the greediness of some anglers who insist on filling their coolers. Bag limits have been instituted in many states to help protect existing stocks. Even without regulations, reasonable fishermen take what they need and turn the rest loose. That way, there will be something to catch the next time and the next and the next.

SPOTTED SEATROUT

Trout and grass are almost synonymous. If you want to locate seatrout, you must first find basins covered with turtle grass. The fish will be in three to ten feet of water, but could be shallower. Plateaus with deeper water on the sides are prime areas. The trout forage in the shallow areas and they are the best places to catch them.

During the colder seasons of the year, the fish either move into deep holes in the marshes, rivers, and bays, or go offshore into the ocean. The best

A basic set of lures for southern flats. Top row includes a chugger and L & S Mirror-Lure. Center: A knife-edge jig used in deep channels along flats' edges, small white bucktail which will take snappers, bonefish, redfish, trout, and a host of other flats species, and the lima bean jig with a few strands of flashy Mylar, which is an all-around jig that can be used in sizes from one-quarter to one ounce.

Lower lure is the barracuda hose lure.

seasons tend to be spring and fall, but there is an excellent summer fishery along the Gulf Coast. Trout are also taken in estuaries along the Atlantic Coast as far north as Chesapeake Bay.

A live shrimp and a popping cork are the most popular method and certainly an effective one. The cork is rigged a few feet up the line from the shrimp. As the rod is moved, the cork acts as a chugger, making a commotion. Trout come topside to see what is happening and eyeball the shrimp. The

Basic jigs that will work on the flats.

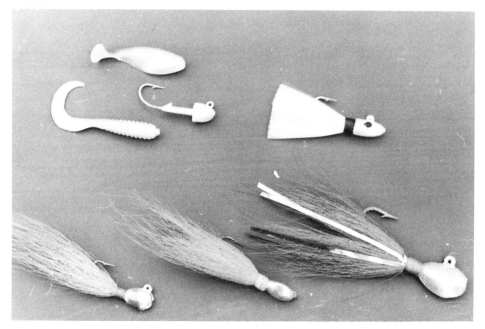

popping cork can also be used with jigs, flies, and other lures. It is nothing more than a noisemaker and attractor.

Since seatrout respond to sound, small lures that pop, dart, or chug will catch their share of fish. Mirror-type plugs are a traditional favorite for this species. Lead-heads with action tails have become increasingly popular. Trout seem to prefer bright colors and anglers oblige with chartreuse, fluorescent red, fluorescent yellow and other shades.

Popping corks are so good that commercial fishermen use them. With a piece of shrimp dangling below the cork, it is popped loudly, drawing seatrout and redfish to the vicinity, where they see the bait and grab it. Here is a nice catch made near Flamingo, Florida Bay, on popping cork and shrimp.

The application of larger eyes on lures is gaining in popularity as more anglers become convinced that big eyes help draw more strikes.

Fly fishermen often tie on keel hooks or create weedless patterns that can be worked through the grass. A 1/0 hook is about average and the fly can be 3 inches or less. Again, bright colors tend to catch more fish. The fly should be worked slowly and just above the bottom. You will find that a sink-tip line or a fast-sinking line will put your fly in the right zone. For those who enjoy top-water sport, try a popping bug on the surface. Trout will come up and hit it like a bass.

Seatrout prefer open areas and are seldom found around the mangroves. If you are in a boat, the best technique is to drift over the flats, casting until you locate the fish. They usually move in schools, so if you catch a couple of fish, you should be in the right place. Throw a marker buoy over the side so you can return to the spot or drop an anchor and hold until the action dies down. Then, start the search pattern once more.

FisHair, an artificial polar bear hair, comes in a number of diameters and is rapidly replacing natural bucktail as a dressing on flies and lures. It is tough, transparent, accepts dyes well, and comes in lengths of from two inches to more than a foot.

Brightly colored flies, especially those that work well just above the bottom of a grassy basin, will take nice trout. Lefty Kreh here unhooks a nice fish that took a flourescent yellow streamer dressed on a Keel hook.

Most fish school according to size. The reason for this is that it is difficult for a small fish to keep up with a large one while swimming. Therefore, if you are catching trout of one size and want bigger fish, you must scout out another school. The chances are remote that huskier specimens will be mixed in with your current one.

REDFISH OR CHANNEL BASS

From Texas to Florida, the redfish frequents shallow, grassy flats with somewhat turbid water. They are back in the marshes along parts of the Gulf Coast or they may probe the oyster bars and mud flats. Redfish feed on shrimp, crabs, or crustaceans, mollusks, and small baitfish.

Since they often swim through or under the thick turtle grass, it may be difficult to spot redfish. The most vivid sign occurs when they are rooting for food and their tails wave above the water. That bronze tail with a few black spots can be detected as far away as 100 yards or more on a calm day.

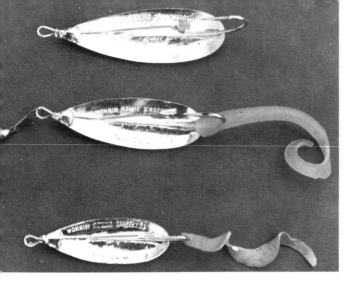

On really grassy flats, or when considerable floating grass makes fishing difficult, no lure beats the Johnson Silver minnow for slithering through the grass. At top is this lure; beneath it is the same lure with a plastic action tail attached, and the bottom lure has a rippled section of pork rind attached. Often, adding one of these will increase strikes.

Lefty Kreh with a #7 fly rod and line and a nice redfish. Note the large black spot on the tail, an identifying characteristic of reds. Some redfish with have several spots on them.

These fish seem to prefer the warmer months, appearing on the flats in greatest abundance from April through October. Along the passes of Louisiana, a run of big redfish occurs from October through December while the smaller reds are holed up in the marshes. North Carolina probably offers the best channel bass fishing for trophy-sized fish. Most are taken in the surf or from boats, but a little-known spring and summer fishery exists on the mud flats in the back bays and estuaries. Few people fish channel bass at that time, thinking that the only activity is in the surf. Another productive area lies along the marsh banks of lower Chesapeake Bay, where big channel bass prowl the flats. Here you may pull up on the back side of an island, walk across, and cast a crab bait over the flats just as the tide is starting to flood.

Channel bass eat a variety of live and dead baits. Some anglers use a mullet head, while others along the Outer Banks prefer crabs, especially in the bays. Farther south, shrimp is the choice bait and is used from Florida to the Mexican border. Those who use artificial lures often tip jigs with a piece of shrimp to appeal to a red's sense of smell.

Redfish have notoriously poor eyesight regardless of size. They will take artificials readily *if* they can see the lure. It is therefore important to cast close to the fish and move the offering slowly. Reds are not as skittish as other species in shallow water and you can drop a lure or a shrimp as close to them as you need.

The main problem in choosing a lure lies in finding something that will ease through the thick grass without hanging up. Weedless spoons with plastic bait tails and jigs with the hook riding up are both popular. Plugs are effective. Try darters that remain on the surface or poppers. On some days, a loud pop will attract fish and at other times it will scare them. You just have to run your own tests.

When they are in very shallow water, as they will be in Florida Bay during a falling tide, you have an excellent shot at them with a fly rod. They are bullish fighters, but do not make long runs nor do they endure for an extensive period, so the tackle can be relatively light. Flies tied on a keel hook are excellent, because they can be retrieved through the grass without hanging up. Another pattern is made by tying several short saddle hackles well back toward the bend of the hook. Then, the entire shank of the hook is dressed with heavily Palmer-tied hackle. You are almost making a dry fly that will stay on top and can be pulled in front of the fish in only six inches of water.

Top-water offerings should be moved very slowly. Remember that it is difficult for a redfish to see the target and it usually homes in by sound or smell. When it does want an artificial, the strike is instantaneous. To keep a natural bait shallow and prevent it from becoming buried in the grass, some anglers use a cork or float just above the hook.

After the smaller reds have moved into the deep holes in the bayous, Gulf coast anglers often fish for the bull reds that range from 25 to 40 pounds. This takes place once the weather gets cold and stretches from late October through December. The technique is to chum the fish in very shallow water.

A skilled fisherman positions himself along the edge of a flat or oyster bar at the bottom of the tide. Spring tides are better because there is a greater flow of water through the passes. Chum obtained from shrimpers and consisting of shrimp, crabs, mollusks, and small bait fish is tossed out where the reds are most likely to pass. Hooks are baited with a variety of offerings, because the fish may opt for crabs one day and shrimp the next. Using a one-half to one-ounce sinker to keep it on the bottom, the bait is cast into the midst of the chum. After that, it's a waiting game. The pickup is very slow and deliberate, but once the line moves off and the hook is set, the battle can be challenging on light gear.

Black drum also frequent these waters and they, too, will put up a tough fight. If nothing happens in one spot, try different areas both inside and along the outside of the barrier islands.

These bigger fish will take artificial lures, but it is much easier to locate them with bait. You might want to keep a couple of outfits rigged, so that if a school moves through, you can cast without having to take the time to rig up.

SNOOK

There is no middle ground. You are either a snook fisherman or you aren't. Those who pursue this salt water counterpart of the largemouth bass develop an addiction that often causes them to pass up a chance at other species. Northern visitors to the tropical flats also like snook fishing, because their quarry exhibits traits similar to the bass. That makes it easier for them to understand the type of cover, feeding situations, ambush points, and lure manipulation necessary.

Snook are found on the flats in parts of Florida, Mexico's Yucatan, the Caribbean, and Central America. They seem to prefer holes or depressions where they lie in wait to ambush an unsuspecting bait fish. Oyster bars form prime terrain, particularly where small creeks empty into a larger basin or estuary.

Falling tide seems to be the best choice for snook fishing in many sectors of its range. It will lie on the open-water side of oyster bars, flats, or obstructions, waiting for its prey to be swept along by the tide. If there are creeks in the area, look for snook at the bottom of the tide in residence where they can pick off bait that lived in the creek until almost the last drop of water drained from it.

During the spring and summer, snook leave the estuaries and go into the open water, working their way along the beachfronts. Most snook catches are made at this time because the fish are easier to locate and approach. A recently concluded study shows that these fish are non-migratory. It was originally believed that they moved along an extensive area of beaches.

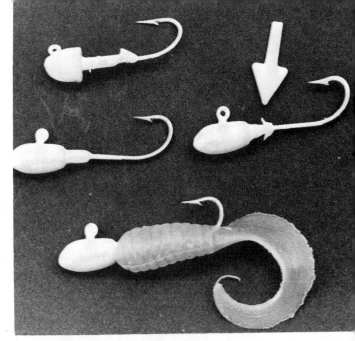

The top jig body has a spur near the hook point that helps hold the soft plastic action tails on the lure. Middle row shows a conventional jig body with no spur, but to the right the same jig has been modified with a penknife, forming two small spurs that will hold the soft tail better. Bottom shows a modified jig head with tail intact.

A nice snook that took a skimmer jig among the mangrove roots of Florida Bay.

Research now shows that the snook return to the same estuary from which they came. Spawning is done outside the home ground during spring tides and the eggs and larvae are swept well back into the estuary where they grow and mature.

In southwestern Florida, the snook population has been steadily declining. Fishing pressure is only part of the problem. The major cause seems to be habitat destruction and alterations in the flow of fresh water through the bottom third of the state. Without mangroves, it is difficult—if not impossible—to maintain any semblance of a viable snook population. They must have that mangrove system in the early stages to survive.

Markers attract big snook, and it's always worth checking them as this angler did.

Snook are particularly susceptible to cold weather and will leave the flats or pack into deeper holes when temperatures drop. During more moderate times, they will take up residence near the depressions or lie along the mangrove keys. At times, you can see them lying under the branches and may even mistake them for barracuda. They prefer water that is a couple of feet or more deep and tend to move farther back during flood tide. On the side of the mangrove islands that faces the prevailing wind, you will usually find a cut or channel close to the key that is deeper than the surrounding water. Snook find these places. Also, if there is a deep hole along one part of the island, that is where the snook will be. Keep in mind that they are always in specific areas and not necessarily distributed evenly along the shoreline. The white holes on flats frequently serve as feeding stations.

Snook are attracted by live bait fish and they will also pick up dead bait off the bottom. Purists hate to admit this fact, but it is true nonetheless. When you are fishing along an oyster bar, yellow bucktails or lead-heads armed with yellow plastic tails work as well as anything. They must be bounced along the bottom with the tide. If they come from the opposite direction, they will not appear natural to the fish. Other colors also work, but snook seem to strike yellow better than most shades.

Top-water offerings or minnow-type plugs will catch snook. Darters are a good choice, as are any of the stick baits that *cha-cha* across the top of the water. Do not pass up the Zara Spook or similar lures. Veteran anglers often switch the approach, using lead-heads for a while, and then going to plugs. The snook, like the bass, is unpredictable and one never knows what it will strike on a given day. You have to keep trying.

The important thing to remember is that the snook takes up residence in specific locations. Points and pockets are prime. If you are fishing a mangrove shoreline or a cluster of oyster bars, seek out the points or other places where the terrain differs slightly from the surrounding area. That is where the snook will be. Snook are like largemouth bass; if you catch a good one from a particular spot, fish it regularly and you should find more.

When snook are on the flats, the accepted technique of fishing them is to make long casts with a bucktail or plug across the yellow sand patches and retrieve across them. If a snook is around, it may hit. This is also an appropriate time to use minnow-type baits and stick baits.

Fly fishing for snook may take the form of blind casting along the mangrove shorelines or of long, searching casts across grass and sand flats where a snook is liable to lie alongside a hole. Yellow, yellow and red, or yellow and grizzly are the best fly colors and patterns should be dressed on hooks from 1/0 to 3/0. Extra-long hooks enable one to build bulkier flies that resemble a good meal. Streamer flies are the most preferable and they should present a good silhouette. There are times when snook will devour a popper on the surface. Sliders made by reversing the popper head may work even better.

Always be on the alert for rays. They swim and stop, pounding the bottom to flush food. Other fish know this and a cast near a cruising ray can often bring a strike from a lurking fish.

OTHER FLATS CRITTERS

Flats fishing must always be viewed as opportunity sport. One never knows what species of fish will appear next in the shallow waters. If your rods are rigged for variety, it is a simple matter to get something to the fish. Who can fault the angler who wants to cast to a particularly large houndfish or takes on a deep-bodied jack crevalle. Bar jacks surprise you from time to time and there is always a chance of finding a husky mutton snapper.

The muttons may be alone up on the flat or along the edge. When they are, assume that they are tougher to approach than the wariest bonefish. If you find a couple shadowing a ray, however, they will more than likely pounce on anything you cast in their direction. Jacks react the same way when they are tailing a ray or shark. That is why it pays to cast to rays, unless you are specializing in a particular species. Sometimes, the fish above their backs are visible, other times they are not.

Vic Dunaway, who knows tropical fishing as well as anyone, often says that he has never met a jack that wasn't hungry. They are agressive feeders and will charge almost anything that moves quickly. Color does not seem to matter, except that our own experience shows they do not hit yellow as well as other hues. When jacks come onto a flat, they may not be following a ray or anything else. Like permit, however, they are constantly on the move and tend to swim very quickly.

In areas where permit fishing is good, you will probably see mutton snappers as well. They seem to like the same sort of terrain. If you can get

One of the pleasures of inshore flats fishing is plugging a shoreline—you never know if you'll get a strike. And then it happens!

near them, they will take a variety of offerings, but the presentation has to be perfect. Don't be surprised if you get refusals from this fish, because they are often fussy when they are in skinny water. You will also discover that they can be more wary than a permit.

There is always some form of marine life visible to anglers who patrol the flats on a regular basis. You may not cast to everything you see and you may exercise the prerogative of selectivity. You will get no argument from us as long as you remember that flats fishing does go beyond bonefish, tarpon, and permit.

12 · Hooking and Landing Fish

REACTING TO A STRIKE ON THE FLATS TAKES MANY forms, depending on the species of fish, the bait or lure, the direction of take, and tackle. One must not only know how to strike each fish, but when to do it. Experience has no substitute, but a series of guidelines may help.

If you have made a transition from fresh water, you will certainly discover soon—if you haven't already—that the denizens of the shallows are tough competitors. They cannot be subdued at will like their freshwater counterparts but will battle with the tenacity and abandon of a barroom brawler. Those anglers who choose simply to hold on and wait it out will invariably lose the fish; or, in rare instances, it may die from old age while still tethered to the hook.

Generally fish are missed on the strike and lost during the fracas because of tackle failure or angler error. Careful preparation will help to eliminate the first reason for defeat. It has been said by experts that fish such as tarpon or bonefish are caught the night before. They are really telling you to take your time in rigging your tackle and to make certain that every element of the equipment is in perfect working order.

If there is a question about the performance of a reel, take it apart and fix it. Replace the drag washers and clean and lubricate the moving parts. Lines must be changed regularly and knots tied with extreme care. A knot in monofilament begins to slip just before it fails, so be sure to tighten every knot securely. You can improve the connections by drawing each one up tightly.

Knowing how to fight a fish helps to eliminate angler error. Couple the correct approach with total concentration and you should begin to land a respectable number of fish. Mistakes in flats fishing are costly. The angler who consistently makes exciting catches invests the time to master the techniques and to keep his tackle in prime condition.

SETTING THE HOOK

You might want to start by reviewing the section on sharpening a hook in Chapter Eight. Every hook should be carefully sharpened. Almost all the species you will encounter in the shallows have relatively tough mouths that make hook penetration difficult. Tarpon and sharks, of course, place an additional burden on the angler when it comes to planting the barb. In fact, some fishermen file the barb down for these species to make it shorter and easier to drive into the mouth.

No matter how or when you set the hook, the line between you and the fish must be tight and the tip of the rod must point directly at your quarry. If you set the hook against a loose line, the effect on fish is negligible. In fact, we urge you to take a spring-scale and actually measure the values when you try to set against a slack line. You also stand a better chance of breaking the line when it is slack. Watch a clerk in a bakery break string after she ties it around a cake box. She holds it in both hands and puts a U in the middle. As she pulls her hands apart and the string suddenly becomes tight, it breaks. The force is enough to overcome the impact resistance of the line.

In a typical strike one waits until the line becomes tight, or reels up the slack, and then lifts the rod with a series of short, sharp jerks in quick succession. The force of each pull should be geared both to the fish you are seeking and to the breaking strength of the line. If you are fishing seatrout, for example, you know that they have tender mouths, so you merely lift the rod sharply. With tarpon, you really have to sock it to them.

In many situations, striking sideways with the rod low and parallel to the water makes more sense. Use short, sharp tugs, but do it with a sideways motion. This involves a natural body rotation that enables you to put force

No hook out of the box is sharp enough to use. To check the point, sharpen it, then touch it against the fingernail. As you draw it across the nail it should dig in—if not, resharpen it.

into the strike. Side-striking has a different effect on bait or lure; the pull becomes relatively straight rather than upward. This means that you could put the hook in the side of the mouth instead of the upper jaw.

Equally significant, a side strike keeps the bait or lure in the vicinity of the fish if you happen to miss. Suppose you are working a darter or top-water lure. Yank upward and the lure flies out of the water, usually landing some distance from the fish and out of its immediate visual range. Keep the rod low and the offering stays right there.

Some of the leading anglers vary this approach slightly. Instead of pulling the rod to set the hook, they simply hold it to one side and parallel to the water, thereby trapping the line against the rod. They let the surge of the fish set the hook, releasing the line as the tarpon starts to move off strongly. We feel that this is the preferred method for tarpon.

For fish with seemingly impregnable jaws, fly fishermen often employ the double haul to set the hook. They pull the rod sideways and parallel to the water with one hand while they tug on the line with the other. With species that have less formidable mouths, one need only lift the rod sharply or tug on the fly line. If you are using delicate tippets and don't want to break them on the strike, lift the rod and let go of the flyline. There will be enough pressure from the rod to bury the barb, but the loose line will cushion the strike and prevent a break-off. Trout fishermen use this slip-strike technique and there is no reason why it should not work whenever a light tippet is involved.

If anglers make a consistent error, it is striking too soon. Fish must expel the water they take into their mouths before they can swallow a bait or lure. A pause before setting the hook enables them to do this. Bonefish and permit have crushers in the backs of their mouths and will toss an offering, including a lead-headed jig, back there to crush it. Setting at once is not critical.

You must also consider the angle. A tarpon follows the lure directly toward the boat. This is called a head-tail take because your quarry is coming straight toward you. If you watch the fish, you will see it open a massive maw and engulf your offering. The natural instinct is to rear back and set the hook. When you do, you miss the fish. A better response is to wait until the tarpon turns away and starts to swim off. That is the time to strike and you will probably do best to sweep the rod parallel to the water.

Some fishermen think about whether a tarpon is going from right to left or left to right when it strikes. They then sweep the rod in the opposite direction, trying to drag the lure into a corner of the fish's mouth.

If you are fishing with a guide and are new to the game, take a moment to ask him how he wants you to strike and when. Timing is critical. A permit picks up a crab and swims off. If you strike too soon, you will probably succeed in pulling the crab away from the fish. If you strike too late, you may reel in a bare hook. We let the line come tight, lean forward until it is really straining, and then set.

FIGHTING A FISH

There is nothing delicate about doing battle with the husky critters of the flats. You know before you ever plant the barb in their jaws that they will run great distances. Tarpon, with few exceptions, will also jump repeatedly. To win in these situations, your tackle must be up to the task and you must think of yourself as a fighter. Boxers know when to circle the ring marking time and when to step in with fists flying. These same tactics apply to whipping a tarpon, shark, permit, bonefish, snook, or anything else.

Preparations must begin before you make the cast. It almost goes without saying that the drag has to be smooth to withstand long runs and the pressure that must be applied. However, you must also set it properly. We maintain that the basic drag should be set relatively light and additional pressure applied with the hands. Regardless of the tackle you are using, we recommend that with the rod pointing directly at a scale you adjust the drag so that it is 15 percent of the breaking strength of the line. If you are using ten-pound-test line, you should have one-and-a-half pounds of drag; if you choose twelve-pound-test line, the drag should be two pounds.

You should also know that when the rod is pointing directly at the fish, the minimum amount of drag is being applied. Once you raise the rod above the horizontal position, additional drag is applied. It is created by the friction of the guides and the arch of the rod. Consider, also, that it takes more pressure to start a reel spool turning than to maintain its turning. We call that starting drag or inertia and it adds to the total.

As a fish runs and the diameter of line remaining on the spool decreases, the drag increases. That is an important point. Most anglers want to tighten the drag if it appears that a fish will take all the line. Actually, the drag should be loosened to compensate for the increased amount of drag. However, if you set the drag initially at 15 percent, there should be enough cushion to withstand the increase without having to reset. We strongly recommend that unless you are very experienced, you do not change the mechanical setting of the drag during the battle. It is too easy to increase the drag too much, and that could cost the fish.

Additional drag can be applied to a reel with your hands and fingers. If you are using spinning tackle, you need only cup the spool with the hand not holding the rod. With a little practice, you can learn to adjust this pressure to fit the situation. Beginners sometimes clamp the spool tightly, breaking the line in the process. The answer is to add just the right amount of pressure without exceeding the limits.

A thumb on the reel spool can put more force into a plug-casting outfit. If the fish has slowed or stopped running, you can press the line against the foregrip or push it aside with your thumb to add even more drag. Fly fishermen can palm the flanges of some reel models, reaching up from underneath to put a finger on the spool, and clamp the line against the foregrip with their fingers. Again, we must caution against applying too much pressure. It must be matched to the fish and to the stage of the fight.

The instant you set the hook, you must expect the fish to run. A bonefish may streak for 150 yards before it pauses at all. Sharks will go even further and tarpon can cover large distances if they don't stop to jump. Your first concern is to minimize the amount of drag on the fish and let the reel spool start turning. You already know that if you point the rod at the fish, the drag will be at the lowest setting. That is precisely what you should do.

Sea fans, coral, and other obstructions on some flats pose a hazard. Bonefishermen have traditionally lifted the rod as high above their heads as they can to keep the line out of the water and to create a sharper angle between rod and fish. If the drag is set exceptionally light, this is fine and probably necessary on some flats. However, the primary task is to get line coming smoothly off the spool. Once that is accomplished, you may lift the rod.

There is no way to stop or snub a fish on that initial run. If you try, you will spend the next few minutes tying a new knot system and re-rigging. The line will pop so quickly that you won't have even an instant for second thoughts. Let the fish go and don't try to stop it even if it seems that all the line will be stripped. In that eventuality, you should have the boat underway to follow or take all the pressure off the fish and hope for the best.

The *instant*—and we emphasize that point—the fish stops running or even pauses to catch its breath, you begin your part of the battle. You must give no quarter. The longer the fish is in the water, the greater your chance of losing it. If you don't care about that, think about the fish. If you plan to release it, you want to turn it loose as quickly as possible. A fish that fights to exhaustion has a poorer chance for survival because of lactic acid buildup in its blood that can eventually poison it. In its weakened state it is also easy prey for a larger fish.

Slack line, except in controlled situations, creates problems. For one thing, it makes it easier for a fish to work the hook or lure free and, for another, it creates a situation where sudden impact can break the line. There should always be a steady strain on the line without any sharp jerks or sudden pulls.

To regain line and bring a fish toward you, you must learn to pump. That is nothing more than lifting the rod and then reeling in the controlled slack created as the rod is lowered. It should be repeated over and over as long as the fish will come your way. If the fish is deep, the pumping action has to be slow and deliberate. Actually, you are trying to lift the fish. On the flats, use a faster pump to bring the fish toward you. Experts often resort to a very short and quick pumping technique, refusing to stop until the fish is alongside the boat or decides to run again.

Slack line is the nemesis of beginners. As they learn to pump, they have a tendency to drop the rod tip faster than the other hand is cranking the reel handle. The result, of course, is slack line which may cause a break-off or enable the fish to free itself. With a little practice, anyone can learn to pump smoothly, lowering the rod as the slack is wound on the reel.

With a light drag setting, you may experience difficulty in pumping, because line may slip every time you lift the rod. That can be overcome easily. Apply additional drag with your hands as outlined above. If the fish should suddenly start to run, simply remove the extra pressure by taking your hand off the reel and dropping the rod tip. When the fish stops, put the pressure back on and keep pumping.

A fish must be fought to the maximum strength of the tackle. If you are using 12-pound-test line, there are times when you will be exerting 11 pounds of pressure. The mistake many beginning anglers make is to "baby" a big fish, thinking, erroneously, that if they take it easy, they have a better chance of landing their quarry. The reverse it true. You either bully a brute or it beats you. Besides, if you pause to rest, the fish will regain its strength faster than you can and you will have to start from square one.

There is a saying that we have promoted for years that where the head of the fish goes, the tail will surely follow. If you are going to beat your adversary, you have to be able to move its head. In deeper water you have to lift, but on the flats the secret is to tack the fish from side to side like a sailboat going upwind. The easiest way to do this is to put side pressure on the fish. Drop the rod so that it is parallel with the water and then pump to one side or the other, keeping the rod parallel. As the fish goes one way, begin pumping in the other direction. That is an excellent way to close the distance and tire a fish.

During every battle, there are a few test points in which the outcome may be in doubt for a few seconds. The fish tries to power off slowly and your task is to turn it. Sometimes, this can be done by reaching forward with the rod and then pulling back. It is almost give and take. Your hand clamps on the reel and you hesitate before yielding line. It is to your advantage to turn the fish, but if the strain becomes critical, remove your hand and let line come off the reel. Try the same procedure again and again until you are consistently successful.

At all times during the battle, you want the fish directly in front of you. Even when you are applying side pressure, the pumping action does not go far and you do not turn too far away from the fish. You want to face your adversary and move with it. If the boat is anchored or staked, you may have to run the gunwale to stay with the fish. The important thing is that you don't find yourself in one spot and the fish somewhere else.

Until now, we have made no mention of what to do when a fish jumps. Tarpon have earned the title of acrobats on the flats, but large barracuda also are capable of greyhounding leaps across the water and snook may jump to some extent. These fish exert a lot less force on the line when they are in the water than when they are in the air. The effects of the water's neutral buoyancy have been negated and a 100-pound tarpon weighs just that when it is airborne. You also have to consider its velocity, or the rate at which it happens to be flying through the atmosphere.

Light-tackle specialists came up with the technique of bowing to the fish many years ago and it is still a valid technique. As soon as the fish starts to break the surface, you push the rod directly at it, lunging forward and stretching. It is as if you held an epee in your hand and were lunging at your opponent. This creates controlled slack line and enables the tackle to withstand the sudden shock of the leap. At the same time, it helps to prevent the fish from landing on a taut line and keeps the hook or lure in the vicinity of the tarpon in the event that it is thrown. Those who have fished tarpon for years acknowledge that the fish sometimes gets re-hooked after it has thrown the lure.

The moment the fish re-enters the water, recover the controlled slack line and apply full pressure once again. It is a matter of give and take. When you can't stop the fish, you must yield; but when you can, you must press forward regardless of how tired you may feel. If you are not exhausted after battling a big fish, you have not been applying maximum pressure or taking advantage of the opportunities.

NEAR THE BOAT

More fish are lost at or near the boat than at any other time. If you have weathered the hook setting and initial run, the next critical moments occur when the battle is nearing its end. We should mention that most fish should be at boatside within 30 minutes and that includes 100-pounders. There are rogue fish that are the exception, but the longer the fight, the more the odds shift from you to the fish.

In the final stages of battle, either the fish surges suddenly and breaks the line on impact or it dives under the boat and cuts the line. The shock-absorbing properties of a line depend to a great degree upon the length of line between you and the fish. When that last dash for freedom occurs close at hand, there is little to absorb the shock. Even the least bit of experience should tell you that any fish is going to dive the instant it sees the boat. Mentally and physically you should be prepared for this. One approach is to loosen the drag slightly when the fish is under control and just before it is brought near the boat.

As your quarry darts away from you, don't try to stop it. Pulling back on the rod only compounds the problem and increases the probability of a break-off. Instead, push the rod at the fish just as you would do if it were jumping. That insures that only the drag that is set on the reel will operate, without the added pressure caused by the bend in the rod. Then, as soon as you can, get the fish back under control and proceed with the finishing touches.

Anticipation is the greatest aid in preventing a fish from dashing under the boat. By using side pressure, try to steer it away and guide it around the boat. If that fails and the fish does go under, shove the rod into the water as far as you can. That allows the line to clear the bottom and the lower unit of the engine. With the tip still in the water, sweep the rod around bow or stern until you and the fish are both on the same side again. Then, continue the battle.

LANDING THE FISH

Long before you are ready to land the fish, you should have decided whether or not you intend to keep it. If you have decided to release your quarry, you must fight it as hard as you can so that you reduce the time it is under stress. We urge you to release as many fish unharmed as you can, regardless of species. No matter what your decision, you must know your quarry before you can land it safely. If an angler does not realize that a fish has sharp teeth, gillrakers, spines, knife-edged gill plates, or other protective devices, he can be painfully injured.

For smaller fish, the net is the most valuable landing tool you have. Even if you are going to release a fish, you can handle it much sooner if you slip a net under it. Otherwise, you have to wait until it is totally exhausted. Have someone place the net in the water at a 45° angle and lead the fish into it. Try always to net head first, since a fish cannot swim backwards and any final lunge will drive it into the mesh. If you intend to keep the fish, lift the net and swing it into the boat with one motion.

If your quarry is to be released, pull the net alongside the boat, but try to keep the fish in the water so that its weight is supported. Handle it firmly but gently. A pair of forceps, pliers, or a hook remover will assist you in getting the hook out. Should the fish have swallowed the hook, do not pull it out. Cut the leader as close to the mouth as you can and release the fish with the hook intact. It will eventually come out and the fish will not be hurt.

Under no circumstances should you hold a fish by its eyes or put your fingers inside its gill covers. Never squeeze a fish you intend to turn loose nor handle it roughly. As soon as the hook is removed, put the fish back into the water and hold it in a swimming attitude. Do not toss it back carelessly. In fact, if you can release the fish in shallow water, it is better, because if the fish starts to sink, you can pick it up again.

If the fish is oriented and in good shape, it may swim off the instant you put it back in the water. Otherwise, and assuming it doesn't have sharp teeth, put your thumb in its lower jaw and hold the tail with your other hand. Move the fish back and forth slowly, forcing water through the gills. This helps the fish to glean oxygen from the water. When it has the strength, it will swim on its own.

Learn how to handle various fish properly. You wouldn't pick up a bluefish with your hand in its mouth, and you'd better be careful of the cutter on a snook. Here's a method of holding a snook preferred by some guides.

Handling a big fish can be dangerous. They have incredible power, particularly in their tails. Never, for example, try to pull a tarpon down if it jumps close to the boat. You could drag it into the boat with you or actually tow the boat under the fish so that it lands inside. The frenzied critter will destroy everything in sight. You already know not to bring sharks into the boat with you. Those jaws earned their reputation.

If a tarpon is to be released, use a short release gaff that can be slipped through its lower jaw *from the inside out*. If you should choose to insert the gaff from the outside, you are asking for trouble, because it tends to cause the tarpon to jump. Although some guides use a wrist rope on a release gaff, we advise against it. If you insist, make sure it has a swivel. A simple, short-handled gaff works fine. Be sure to triangulate the point so that it will penetrate easily. Once the gaff is slipped into the mouth of the fish, the point should be pinned against the gunwale. You can expect the fish to shake and rattle, so keep a good grip on the handle. When the lure is deep, use a tool to get it out or leave it there. Reaching down into that cavernous mouth can be dangerous if the fish decides to break loose.

Resist gaffing any fish you don't want. The release gaff through the skin in the lower jaw causes the least amount of damage and does not seem to hurt the fish. If you do want to boat a big tarpon or put a gaff in a shark, you must have the right equipment. This is serious business. The standard "killer" gaff is eight feet long and has a hand-honed hook with a six- or eight-inch gap. The point should be protected with a piece of tubing when not in use. Any gaff that has a spring-type protector can be a problem. If the line catches in the spring, you will never get it free and you may lose the fish.

On a tarpon, you must penetrate the big scales and that is not easy. Some guides prefer to reach across the back when they gaff the fish, while others would rather come from the underside just behind the gills, turning the fish over to deprive it of its normal swimming attitude. It is a matter of choice. The gaff should be kept out of the fish's vision until the precise moment of insertion. Never reach in front of the leader with the gaff and never make a swipe at the fish.

When releasing any fish that doesn't have dangerous teeth, and if the fish must be revived a bit, grip the lower lip as shown in the drawing, and grasp the tail. Rock the fish underwater back and forth rather vigorously, which will force water through the mouth and gills and quickly revive most fish.

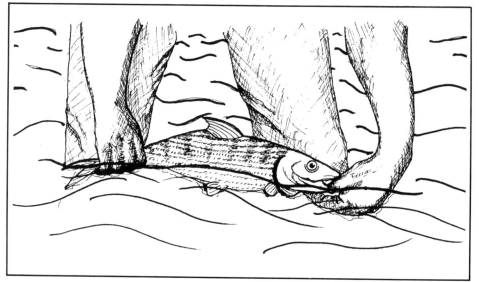

A jack crevalle held in this manner doesn't move.

Two large gaffs, properly stored so they are quickly available yet stored where they can't harm anyone.

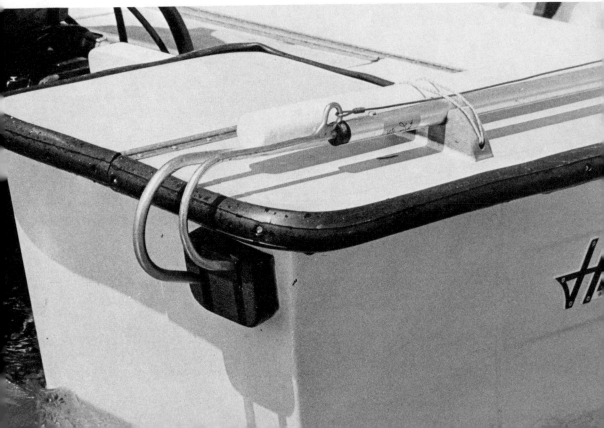

Remember that the gaff is a lever and it works two ways. More than one strong guide has been vaulted out of the boat by a tarpon and others have been dragged the length of a skiff by a fish that could not be stopped. When you hit the fish, you want to penetrate muscle. The stroke must be timed and it must be as positive as you can make it. Some experts actually hurl themselves across the boat and away from the fish to help drive the point.

To gaff successfully, you must be between the angler and the fish, but the angler must also be able to see everything that is happening. If he backs off too far, he may not be able to react to the sudden movements of his quarry. Once the gaff has penetrated, drop to your knees. It will help to keep you in the boat.

There are moments during the fight itself when you may be able to gaff the fish. They do not last long and one has to be ready to capitalize on them. If you are, you can cut the battle short on a record fish. We would also suggest that when you gaff a fish, you know where you want to put it in the boat and that the place is prepared. Fish have been known to come off gaffs if allowed to remain in the water.

Finally, if you gaff a shark, remember that most of them have a habit of twisting around and around. They will turn a gaff right out of your hands and skin your palms in the process. If you are going to gaff sharks, you need a gaff with revolving grips that will turn when the fish does.

13 · Fishing Other Flats

SHALLOW WATER FISHING HAS NEVER BEEN LIMITED to the tropics. It takes place regularly in many of the bays and estuaries that dot our coastlines. Species such as striped bass, bluefish, common weakfish, red and black drum, and the crowd-pleasing flounder are the source of continuous action in thin water. The problem with most of the non-tropical flats is lack of water clarity. Usually, there is enough turbidity to make visibility difficult. One cannot scan vast distances under the surface or spot fish before the cast is made. Instead, long, searching casts are made to locate the quarry by chance. The alternative is bottom fishing with bait.

Working these shallow regions takes a great deal of skill coupled with local knowledge. The tides are just as important as they are on the bonefish flats, because they determine when fish will be there and where they can be found. Without the right stage of the tide, the flat may be totally devoid of game fish. If you fish a shallow water sector regularly, take the time to study the effects of tidal conditions. Do not overlook the spring tides or the neaps. More than one angler has been surprised to learn after many years of fishing an area that the fish congregate where he never expected them to be during certain tidal stages.

When you are learning about a new place, pick one section of it and work it very carefully. Learn as much as you can about it and the knowledge will pay off. That lesson was burned into our memory by a guide who refused to leave a shallow area where we were awaiting the arrival of big bluefish. Schools of blues were churning the surface to a froth in deeper water and we could see other boats racing for the bonanza. "When the tide falls a little more, our fish will be here," the skipper stated confidently, ignoring our request to join the fleet in the chase. "Besides," he continued, "we'll have fish ranging from twelve pounds up and those are only 3- to 4-pounders." We stayed and he was right. He knew the area well and was not about to be pulled out of position by the allure of a fleeting moment.

WORKING THESE FLATS

The pushpole has yet to be discovered along many sections of the coast. Anglers seem content to allow the wind or tide to push the boat. In a few places, fishermen may use a sea anchor or drag chain to slow the drift, but that is the extent of the effort. A few owners of bass boats have electric motors and sometimes use these for positioning.

Fish are as skittish about noise and disturbances in turbid water as they are when you can read a newspaper lying on the bottom. When the water is murky, however, you cannot see the fish, so you have no way of knowing they are there or of monitoring their response to sound. If anglers could see a school clear the flats in response to an outboard, they would mend their ways in a hurry.

The same careful method of approaching the flats in the tropics applies to colder climes. You will probably start the drift upwind or upcurrent. Run well outside of the flats and throttle down while you are still in deeper water. Plan your drift a distance above where you expect the fish to be. Then, motor very, very slowly without changing rpms until you are in that exact position. Secure the engine and start fishing.

When you have finished the drift, start the motor and put-put out to the channel. Only then should the throttle be pushed forward for another run. Make a wide swing around the area you are going to fish and enter the flats again from beyond the position of the fish.

Whether you can spot your quarry or not, a flat should be worked systematically. Fish may be deeper or shallower than you suspect and in one sector or another. Choose landmarks to help you get precise bearings. Then, each drift can be farther in one direction or another. As soon as you start catching fish, mark the spot so that you can come back. In some places, it may pay to anchor, but in other types of fishing you have to drift through and pole back a second, third, and fourth time.

By fanning casts, you can cover an even broader area on each drift. You will discover that the direction you cast helps to determine the action on your lure. If you cast downdrift, you don't get as much action on top water, because slack is always being created and you are losing some of the surface tension. With bucktails and lead-heads, you must retrieve quickly just to keep up with the lure. The best direction is usually at right angles to the drift. That way, you are working the lure across the current for a more realistic action. If two anglers are fishing, each one can take a section from the beam of the boat to bow or stern. Quartering the casts also helps.

The alert and observant angler has the advantage over those who merely cast blindly. Even when you cannot see through the water, there are signs to look for. Sometimes, it is possible to see breaking bluefish or to detect the swirls of a feeding striper. Fish in very shallow water create wakes as they move. Cross ripples are just as valid under cloudy conditions as they are when the water is clear. Birds feeding or schools of bait fish are other signs. A flat that has activity on it will entice predators.

Anglers fishing the waters along the northeast coast often wade for striped bass, weakfish, and blues. This wading may be done at night as well as early and late in the day. Although some anglers prefer fishing alone, it is a good idea from a safety standpoint always to wade with a partner. Strong tides and rips or unseen dropoffs may prove to be a hazard. At the very least it is comforting to know that help is nearby.

STRIPED BASS

There is a certain reverence in the voice of an addict when he talks about his beloved striped bass. This fish oozes appeal and lures anglers to the waterfront in every type of weather. Early in the season, the striper probes the flats in search of a meal. The fish are sluggish on the East Coast until water temperatures climb, but they will take a bloodworm or sandworm fished on the bottom in a few feet of water. Those who favor the use of artificials must employ a slow retrieve with a lead-head or plug that stays down.

As the season progresses and water temperatures rise, the fish become much more active. Their presence on the flats depends on the bait supply and the temperature of the water. In places such as the bays of the New Jersey coast, linesiders probe the flats during the springtime and anglers either wade for them or fish from small boats. Similar activity takes place in the Chesapeake Bay and throughout New England.

Later in the year, the best fishing occurs early in the morning and again in the evening just before dark. Striper enthusiasts also fish through the hours of darkness and do well. When the bait starts moving during the fall of the year, striped bass gather in the estuaries and work their way along the coasts following the food source. Eventually, they return to the deep pockets in the bays and rivers to winter. Throughout their active period, striped bass can be taken on a variety of lures and fly patterns.

When the fish are in the shallows, you must use a stealthy approach, making long casts from the boat as it drifts over the spots. You also have the option of wading for the fish. Remember to cast at right angles to the drift or at least quarter those casts to enjoy the benefits of a longer retrieve. At times, the fish will break water and feed on the surface. If you keep scanning the water around you, you will probably see such activity. Look for birds wheeling and diving as telltale indicators of action below.

In some areas, chumming with ground-up clams or crabs brings schools of striped bass within casting range. They may also be fished with bait in these situations. The necessary conditions are a running tide to carry the chum and the right location to lure the fish out of deeper water.

Fishing the flats for striped bass has become a popular pastime in California's San Francisco Bay, Half Moon Bay to the south, and Tomales Bay to the north. Much of these bays are covered with mud flats and bait species such as herring, jack smelt, and anchovies seek a sanctuary from predators in the shallows. The striped bass will pursue the bait even though their backs are almost out of water.

Not every flat is productive and it helps if you have local knowledge or know someone who does. At times you may spot waking fish or even surface swirls, but the sport is primarily blind casting and you have to know where to do it to increase the odds. Pilings, old docks, radar towers, and other structures and obstructions may prove to be striper hangouts and it is often possible to anchor upcurrent of these and fan the area with casts.

Lead-headed jigs work well and so do a variety of plugs. Fly fishermen love this territory, because they can catch big fish. Local experts have designed a series of bulky fly patterns such as Dan Blanton's Whistler series or Ed Givens's Barred-N-Black that seem to lure fish in the murky water. These anglers reason that a fly that has bulk creates more underwater sound and is easier for a striped bass to locate. Using sinking shooting heads, they make extremely long casts, insisting that the distance of retrieve is vital in catching fish.

There are some big stripers in the shallow flats of bays along the West Coast. Here Dan Blanton, West Coast expert fly rodder, lifts a good fish into the boat.

Don Peters with a nice bluefish taken on fly in Chesapeake Bay shallows in the spring, when fish topping 17 pounds move into two to five feet of water to feed.

August and September are the prime months for striped bass, but the fishing remains good through November. Very early morning and late evening are perhaps the best times, but fish can be caught during the day in selected places when a strong tide is flowing. In this case, neap tides are better than spring tides, because many areas are left bare when the spring tides and winds together drive off the water.

In many parts of its range and particularly on the East Coast, the striped bass is in serious difficulty. Unless successful management practices are implemented and enforced, the survival of this great game fish is in question.

BLUEFISH

Bluefish are voracious feeders and highly successful predators. They are constantly on the move, searching for food sources and comfortable conditions. Few people realize, for example, that you can catch bluefish during the winter months on the deeper flats in Florida's Biscayne Bay and throughout the Keys. They are found in Lake Worth off Palm Beach and farther up the coast. There is no telling where a bluefish will appear and the shallows should be checked regularly.

Each May, when water temperatures range between 62° and 72°, blues that weigh in the double figures swarm into a couple of feet of water near the Bay Bridge in the Chesapeake Bay. They only stay there for a few weeks, providing outstanding action for top water lures and flies. The fish work the tides, moving in and out with them. Action is better on high water than low tide. Anglers use small skiffs to reach the fish and they drift quietly, making long casts and working surface lures to find the fish.

Later in the season, smaller blues replace the big ones, but there may be activity over the flats for months at a time. The same phenomenon occurs in other bays and estuaries along the coast. Big fish move in for a couple of weeks and are gone. By August, most of the flats are filled with the year's young snappers that please anglers of every age when fished with very light tackle.

The bluefish will strike almost any type of bait or lure and its dentures are legendary. However, you will catch a lot more fish if you use 50- to 80-pound monofilament instead of wire leaders in clear water. If you do opt for stainless steel wire, use a short trace only a few inches long. That is much better than a long piece.

Many flats harbor bluefish throughout the summer months. You must know the tides and where to be. If you can acquire that local knowledge, you will have a lot of fun using a variety of tackle combinations. During the fall months, blues will swarm back along the coast and make forays into the bays. They feed heavily on migrating bait fish and work their way south for the winter. That is also a good time to find them on some flats.

Casting tackle is ideal for bluefish. Fly fishermen can have a great deal of sport with this species. They will hit either streamer flies or poppers on the surface. The best approach is to locate them with spinning or plug gear before switching to fly. If they are in the area, you can expect them to strike readily. When they don't, you know something is wrong and it pays to change your tactics.

WEAKFISH

A cousin of the spotted seatrout, the weakfish has been staging a remarkable comeback in many northern waters. During the spring of the year, Delaware Bay is a hot spot and plenty of action takes place out on Long Island. This fish also is found in New England waters and in the gaps in between. They have the same soft mouth as the seatrout, but will take up residence on sandy bottoms and mud flats as well as grass-coated areas.

Action tails on lead-heads are perhaps the most popular type of lure for weakfish. Anglers bounce an offering along the bottom using light lines. Bright colors seem to produce better results than the dark ones. The fish will also strike plugs and even hit surface lures on occasion. Fly rodders have found a friend in the weakfish on many of the flats, particularly those out on Long Island. Much of the fishing is done at night and fly fishermen wade for the fish.

Streamer flies tied on 1/0 or 2/0 hooks do well and fluorescent colors are effective. Yellows and reds or combinations of these catch fish. Some anglers are also using chartreuse.

The late Lew Jewett holds one of the many types of snappers and groupers that inhabit the coastal waters of Baja, Mexico.

When the weakfish are on the flats and cooperating, most of the local newspapers carry reports in their outdoor columns. It is easy to pinpoint the heart of the activity. These fish will also show up without warning near schools of bluefish. They may hang just below the blues so that if you can get a lure down through the choppers, you may find weakfish below.

SUMMER FLOUNDER

The summer flounder, or fluke as it is called in some places, ranks as one of the most popular coastal species. Although it is found in the ocean, it is particularly abundant along the mud and sand flats of virtually every coastal estuary within its range. Not noted for its fighting ability, the flounder still provides good sport and is among the tastiest fish on the table.

Because it buries in the mud and hugs the bottom, the flounder is not as easily frightened by noises on the flats. In fact, anglers troll very, very slowly for them along marshy areas and soft flats. The primary methods of fishing for them are to drift a flat or anchor and cast. When bait fishing, a sinker is used to keep the offering on the bottom and a relatively light leader about three feet long puts the bait where it can be seen.

Favorite baits include strips of squid, killifish, spearing, sand launce, and combinations of these. It is not uncommon to put a piece of squid and a killie on the same hook.

The key to catching flounder lies in keeping the sinker on the bottom. Choosing the right sinker is therefore vital. You want just enough weight to hold the bait down, but you also want it to roll around or move with the current. Some anglers lift the rod to drag the bait across the bottom in short moves. A few bright red beads and a Colorado spinner may increase the response. The strike is less than spectacular and often you only feel weight when you start to reel. If the bait stops or the sinker seems to hang, it may be a fish.

Most people don't realize that the flounder is an aggressive feeder and will come off the bottom to take a lure or fly. They are caught on bucktails bounced along the bottom and also on plugs that probe the bottom layer. Fly fishermen use streamer flies effectively, but they also have caught flounder on poppers. The only time poppers should be used is when the flounder are in a couple of feet of water. They will come to the top to hit a popper if it is retrieved slowly.

OTHER SPECIES

Flats fishermen also have the opportunity to catch other species, such as red and black drum. Much of this fishing takes place from Delaware Bay down through the Carolinas. Both varieties of drum will prowl the shallow flats and may be taken with crabs, mullet heads, and other offerings. They also hit artificial lures and take flies readily if they see them.

Finding the fish can be difficult without knowledge of the routes they take in their search for food. Usually, they invade the mud flats on a flooding tide and work around points of islands or near the edges of deeper channels. They will invariably be close to deeper water. Fishing is done from drifting or anchored boats. In some parts of the Chesapeake, anglers come up on the back side of an island and use surf rods to get a bait out on the fishable side.

The shallows have long held an attraction for many species of fish. They know instinctively that the bait supply lives in these waters and that a predator must foresake its natural instincts for cover to go where the food happens to be. For the flats fisherman, it is a matter of remaining alert and taking advantage of every opportunity. It is surprising how much, with a little investigation, one can learn about the various coastal species that invade the flats at some time or other.

14 · A Look Ahead

IF YOU HAVE COME THIS FAR WITH US, YOU KNOW THAT fishing the shallow flats holds a special fascination and answers angling needs better than any other facet of the sport. Flats fishing is a one-on-one confrontation in which an angler stalks his quarry before he makes the presentation. Equally important, all of the action takes place in a fragile ecosystem where one often can see the bottom and the variety of life it supports.

Catching fish is only one aspect of the endeavor. You develop an appreciation for the beauty of the environment and its battle to survive. There may be days on the flats when you go fishless and still come away with a feeling of satisfaction simply from being there. The scenery never seems to tire the eyes or the mind.

Those of us who have pursued flats fishing for more years than we care to admit are concerned. Over the seasons, we have observed a deterioration in fishing for some species and a consequent need to probe farther and farther into the remaining pristine areas. That doesn't mean that you can't or won't catch fish, but the bonefish schools are a bit smaller and there are fewer snook around than there once were.

A growing legion of anglers gravitates to salt water fishing and the shallow flats. Many look to the marine scene as an escape from overcrowded streams and poor fresh water sport. Others come because the challenges of light tackle are greater in thin water than anywhere else. No one can blame these fishermen for their decision nor should any effort be made to limit flats fishing.

The problem is that newcomers view the salt as an endless well. It is not and never was. Far-sighted people talk in terms of stocking oceans to support the increased fishing pressure. Trial balloons have already been sent aloft and one suspects that more efforts are on the drawing boards. Whether or not successful stocking techniques will be developed and implemented remains to be seen, but you can bet that it will be an expensive process.

If the tarpon, bonefish, or permit had commercial value and were sold as food fishes, the situation today would be bleak. The saving grace is that most

157

of these species are released unharmed and few people pursue them for food. Within certain areas of its range, the bonefish is eaten, but not in the United States where the pressure is greatest.

Flats and estuaries are among the richest lands in the world. They should be treasured and protected and yet they are not. Developers view an estuary as an unbuilt housing project or a barrier wall of condominiums. Systematic destruction of our coastal estuaries ranks as the foremost threat to fishing facing us today. Without the estuary, most game fish and all of the flats species cannot survive. When populations diminish, it is often because the larvae and juveniles cannot make it; they require estuaries, and this habitat is being destroyed by uncaring people.

In the lower half of Florida, mangroves are being eliminated at an incredible rate. It is the root system of the mangroves that filters the water and makes it clear. These same roots are a haven for countless juveniles. Efforts are underway to stop this destruction and start a rebuilding process. When concrete seawalls replace the mangroves, there is no way fish are going to survive.

Florida is also plagued with water problems, especially the diversion of fresh water from its natural destination. The Everglades are really a broad, slow-flowing river that moves through the saw grass to Florida Bay. This influx of fresh water is vital to both bait and game fish species. Diversionary controls by water management commissions have upset the balance of nature and threaten the very existence of the Everglades and of fishing in Florida Bay. It is one of the great nursery grounds and it is being destroyed.

The conflict between sport and commercial interests will always be present. Concessions must be made on both sides, but when netters move into places like Florida Bay and virtually eliminate the bait supply, it is a problem that cannot be overlooked. After an absence of several years, grass started to take root on the bottom of Maryland's Susquehanna flats at the head of Chesapeake Bay. This return of habitat brought striped bass back into the area. The netters were right behind. Not only did they take the rockfish, but they tore up much of the new grass in the process, eliminating the habitat that held the fish in the first place.

If you do not think conditions are changing, look at the policies of the guides in the Florida Keys. A few years ago, they brought in all kinds of fish and either used them for food or hung them on racks to attract new customers. Today, those same guides are in the vanguard, asking to have bag limits placed on several species and turning fish loose automatically. Now, it is a matter of survival.

Those who have fished barracuda in the same area for a few decades will tell you with sadness how the average size of the fish has decreased over the years. There was a time, however, when every barracuda was killed and dragged back to the dock and displayed before being tossed in a garbage can. These practices should not and cannot continue. Every fish is becoming

It's important that we release more fish in salt water. The increasing numbers who are using the fishery make it imperative that we put back most of our catch.

increasingly valuable in the water. A dead fish can never spawn again and it is becoming more difficult for fish to survive.

For those who doubt the effect of sport fishing pressure, consider that there are at least twice as many fishing guides in the Florida Keys as there were 20 years ago. All of them have better boats than they did. Anglers now use polarized glasses, improved tackle, more effective lures, and the fishermen themselves are much more knowledgeable and experienced. Things have to be getting tougher for the fish.

If we sound upset, it is because of our personal love for the flats and everything on them. We can remember what it was like and can only hope that fishing in the shallows will continue and even improve in years to come. Flats fishing is an unforgetable experience and we would like you and every other angler to gain the same measure of enjoyment from it as we do. It is only possible if all of us become concerned.

We all must begin caring. When it is time to fight for the preservation of the flats, all of us must join the battle. Leaving it to the other guy may not get the job done. On an individual basis, we must vow to protect the environment every time we are on it. The ecosystem is extremely fragile. Above all, we should release every unwanted fish unharmed and take only what we need. If everyone is conscientious, government-imposed bag limits will not be necessary.

Unless all of us accept the challenge and the responsibility of caring for the flats, estuaries, and the species of both bait fish and game fish that depend on them for survival, this form of fishing as we know it and love it will not endure.